W9-BJF-593

Teaching Students With Autism Spectrum Disorders

This book is dedicated to my wife, Jackie, and my two children, Jacqueline and Scott, who provide me with the love and purpose for undertaking projects that I hope will enhance the lives of others. My life has been blessed by their loving presence. I also dedicate this book to my parents, who provided me with the secure and loving foundation from which to grow; my sister, Carol, who makes me smile and laugh; and my brother-in-law, George, who has always been a positive guiding light in my professional journey.

—R.P.

This book is dedicated to my wife, Anita, and two children, Collin and Brittany, who give me the greatest life imaginable. The long hours and many years it took to finish this book would never have been possible without the support of my loving wife. Her constant encouragement, understanding, and love provide me with the strength I need to accomplish my goals. I thank her with all my heart. I also dedicate this book to my parents, who have given me support and guidance throughout my life. Their words of encouragement and guidance have made my professional journey a rewarding and successful experience.

—G.G.

A STEP-BY-STEP GUIDE FOR EDUCATORS

Teaching Students With Autism Spectrum Disorders

ROGER PIERANGELO ~ GEORGE GIULIANI

CORWIN PRESS
A SAGE Company
Thousand Oaks, CA 91320

Copyright © 2008 by Corwin Press

Photos courtesy of Susan Stokes. Used with permission.

All rights reserved. When forms and sample documents are included, their use is authorized only by educators, local school sites, and/or noncommercial or nonprofit entities that have purchased the book. Except for that usage, no part of this book may be reproduced or utilized in any form or by any means, electronic or mechanical, including photocopying, recording, or by any information storage and retrieval system, without permission in writing from the publisher.

For information:

Corwin Press
A SAGE Company
2455 Teller Road
Thousand Oaks, California 91320
www.corwinpress.com

SAGE India Pvt. Ltd.
B 1/I 1 Mohan Cooperative
   Industrial Area
Mathura Road, New Delhi 110 044
India

SAGE Ltd.
1 Oliver's Yard
55 City Road
London EC1Y 1SP
United Kingdom

SAGE Asia-Pacific Pte. Ltd.
33 Pekin Street #02-01
Far East Square
Singapore 048763

Printed in the United States of America

Library of Congress Cataloging-in-Publication Data

Pierangelo, Roger.
Teaching students with autism spectrum disorders: a step-by-step guide for educators/ Roger Pierangelo, George Giuliani.
      p. cm.
Includes bibliographical references and index.
ISBN 978-1-4129-1707-0 (cloth: acid-free paper)
ISBN 978-1-4129-1708-7 (pbk.: acid-free paper)
   1. Autistic children—Education—United States. 2. Learning disabled children—Education—United States. I. Giuliani, George A., 1938- II. Title.

LC4718.P54 2008
371.94—dc22   2008004900

This book is printed on acid-free paper.

         10   11   12   10   9   8   7   6   5   4   3   2

Acquisitions Editor:	David Chao
Editorial Assistant:	Mary Dang
Production Editor:	Eric Garner
Copy Editor:	Paula L. Fleming
Typesetter:	C&M Digitals (P) Ltd.
Proofreader:	Charlotte Waisner
Cover Designer:	Michael Dubowe
Graphic Designer:	Lisa Riley

Contents

Preface

Autism spectrum disorder (ASD) is a developmental disorder of neurobiological origin that can have lifelong effects on social interaction, ability to communicate ideas and feelings, imagination, and establishment of relationships. ASD varies in severity of symptoms, age of onset, and association with other disorders, such as mental retardation, language disability, and epilepsy. The manifestation also varies across children and time. No two individuals with ASD are alike, even if they have the same diagnosis. ASD affects approximately four times more boys than girls. According to the National Research Council (2001), "There is no single behavior that is always typical of ASD and no behavior that would automatically exclude an individual child from a diagnosis of ASD, even though there are strong and consistent commonalities, especially in social deficits" (p. 11).

Leo Kanner identified characteristics of ASD in 1943. After more than 60 years, these characteristics are still current. They include (a) problems in relating to people and situations; (b) speech and language problems; (c) developmental delays; (d) problems in relating to environmental changes; and (e) stereotypic, repetitive actions and other peculiar motor movements (Simpson & Zionts, 2000).

The overall goal of educational programs for all students, including students with ASD, is a life with independence and functioning within the community. Reaching this goal requires an education based on the individual needs of the child/student. Setting the individual goals for each child requires realistic assessment of present levels of ability, as well as identification of learning deficits. In other words, what can the child with ASD do now, what skills does the child excel in, what skills can be enhanced, and what skills does the student need to be able to seek employment and live in the community in adulthood? Is there improvement in the child's social and language development? Are negative behaviors being addressed? What kind of program does it take to accomplish the overall goal?

In general, we know that we must structure the classroom environment so the educational program is consistent and predictable for the student. Children with ASD are less confused and learn better in that environment. They also learn better with information presented visually as well as verbally. Insofar as is appropriate, children with ASD should have opportunities to interact with nondisabled peers who can provide models of appropriate behavior, language, communication, social, and play skills.

Students with ASD should also have training in community living skills and vocational skills at the earliest possible age. They need to be taught how to interact with others and be provided opportunities to develop relationships with other students. Teaching safety habits, such as crossing the street or asking for help when needed, is critical to developing independence. Learning to make simple purchases and to handle money is another example of a needed skill. All of these skills may be difficult, in varying degrees, for the student with ASD to learn. However, ongoing assessment of abilities along with individualized education programs will facilitate the achievement of maximum independence for each child with ASD.

The importance of family involvement in the educational program is paramount. Programs developed with the parents to carry over learning activities, experiences, and approaches from school to the home and community will facilitate generalization of those skills. Generalization to home and community is essential for each child with ASD to develop maximum independence and integration into the community. Also, specialized adult support services in employment and living arrangements are available to support youth and adults with ASD in living and working with varying degrees of independence in the community.

Teaching Students with Autism Spectrum Disorders: A Step-by-Step Guide for Educators will provide an overview of ASD and numerous strategies essential to implementing effective educational programs for these students. After reading *Teaching Students with Autism Spectrum Disorders: A Step-by-Step Guide for Educators*, you should understand the following:

- Characteristics of children with ASD
- Types of ASDs
- Eligibility criteria for children with ASD
- Effective interventions for young children with ASD
- Creating quality educational programs for children with ASD

- Collaborating with parents
- Effective programming for young children with ASD
- Teaching students with ASD: Instructional approaches
- Teaching students with ASD: Strategies for classroom management
- Teaching students with ASD: Strategies for communication development
- Teaching students with ASD: Strategies for social skills
- Teaching students with Asperger syndrome
- Assistive technology for students with ASD
- Behavior and discipline issues for students with ASD
- Facilitating inclusion of children with ASD
- Transition planning for students with ASD

Acknowledgments

We wish first to thank and acknowledge Susan Stokes, an autism spectrum disorder (ASD) consultant, who has done significant research in the field of ASD. Under a contract with Wisconsin's Cooperative Education Service Agency 7 (CESA 7) and funded by a discretionary grant from the Wisconsin Department of Public Instruction, Ms. Stokes wrote the following articles, which she granted us permission to disseminate in various sections throughout this book: "Assistive Technology for Children With Autism," "Children With Asperger Syndrome: Characteristics/Learning Styles and Intervention Strategies," "Effective Programming for Young Children With Autism (Ages 3–5)," and "Structured Teaching: Strategies for Supporting Students With Autism." We are greatly appreciative of her granting permission to use her information and photographs, as her outstanding work sheds great light on the field of ASDs.

In the course of writing this book, we have encountered many professional and outstanding sites. Those resources have contributed and continue to contribute invaluable sources of information, support, guidance, and education to parents, students, and professionals in the area of special education. Although we have accessed many worthwhile sites, we especially thank and acknowledge the following: the National Dissemination Center for Children with Disabilities, the New York State Department of Education, Centers for Disease Control (CDC), the Ministry of Education: Alberta Education, and the National Institutes of Health—all for their excellent research in the field.

Dr. Roger Pierangelo and Dr. George Giuliani extend sincere thanks to David Chao, Allyson Sharp, Paula Fleming, and Mary Dang at Corwin Press. Their constant encouragement and professionalism made this project a very worthwhile and rewarding experience. We also thank the following for their professional editorial contributions to this book:

Caroline I. Magyar, PhD
Associate Professor of Pediatrics
University of Rochester
Autism Spectrum Disorder
    Program
Rochester, NY

G. Richmond Mancil, PhD
Assistant Professor
Autism Specialist
Department of Child, Family,
    and Community Sciences
University of Central Florida
Orlando, FL

Vicki McFarland
Special Education Director
Learning Matters Educational
    Group
Glendale, AZ

Ronda Schelvan
Special Education Teacher
District Autism Consultant
Hathaway Elementary School
Vancouver, WA

Tina Stanton-Chapman
Assistant Professor
Curry School of Education
University of Virginia
Charlottesville, VA

Roger Pierangelo: I extend thanks to the following: the faculty, administration, and staff of the Department of Graduate Special Education and Literacy at Long Island University; Ollie Simmons, for her friendship, loyalty, and great personality; the students and parents of the Herricks Public Schools whom I have worked with and known over the past 35 years; the late Bill Smyth, a truly gifted and "extraordinary ordinary" man; and Helen Firestone, for her influence on my career and her tireless support.

George Giuliani: I extend sincere thanks to all of my colleagues at Hofstra University in the School of Education and Allied Human Services. I am especially grateful to those who have made my transition to Hofstra University such a smooth one, including Maureen Murphy (dean), Darra Pace (chairperson), Frank Bowe, Diane Schwartz (graduate program director of early childhood special education), Daniel Sciarra, Gloria Wilson, Mary McDonald, Elfreda Blue, Laurie Johnson, Joan Bloomgarden, Jamie Mitus, Estelle Gellman, Holly Seirup, Adele Piombino, Marjorie Butler, and Eve Byrne. I also thank my brother and sister, Roger and Claudia; mother-in-law, Ursula Jenkeleit; sisters-in-law, Karen and Cindy; and brothers-in-law, Robert and Bob. They have provided me with encouragement and reinforcement in all of my personal and professional endeavors.

About the Authors

Roger Pierangelo, PhD, is an associate professor in the Department of Special Education and Literacy at Long Island University. He has been an administrator of special education programs; served for 18 years as a permanent member of Committees on Special Education; has over 30 years of experience in the public school system as a general education classroom teacher and school psychologist; and serves as a consultant to numerous private and public schools, PTA, and SEPTA groups. Dr. Pierangelo has also been an evaluator for the New York State Office of Vocational and Rehabilitative Services and a director of a private clinic. He is a New York State–licensed clinical psychologist, a certified school psychologist, and a Board Certified Diplomate Fellow in Student and Adolescent Psychology and Forensic Psychology. Dr. Pierangelo is the executive director of the National Association of Special Education Teachers (NASET) and an executive director of the American Academy of Special Education Professionals (AASEP). He also holds the office of vice president of the National Association of Parents with Children in Special Education (NAPCSE).

Dr. Pierangelo earned his BS from St. John's University, MS from Queens College, Professional Diploma from Queens College, PhD from Yeshiva University, and Diplomate Fellow in Student and Adolescent Psychology and Forensic Psychology from the International College of Professional Psychology. Dr. Pierangelo is a member of the American Psychological Association, New York State Psychological Association, Nassau County Psychological Association, New York State Union of Teachers, and Phi Delta Kappa.

Dr. Pierangelo is the author of multiple books by Corwin Press, including *The Big Book of Special Education Resources* and the *Step-by-Step Guide for Educators* series.

George Giuliani, JD, PsyD, is a full-time tenured associate professor and the director of Special Education at Hofstra University's School of Education and Allied Human Services in the Department of Counseling, Research, Special Education, and Rehabilitation. Dr. Giuliani earned his BA from the College of the Holy Cross, MS from St. John's University, JD from City University Law School, and PsyD from Rutgers University, the Graduate School of Applied and Professional Psychology. He earned Board Certification as a Diplomate Fellow in Student and Adolescent Psychology and Forensic Psychology from the International College of Professional Psychology. Dr. Giuliani is also a New York State–licensed psychologist and certified school psychologist and has an extensive private practice focusing on students with special needs. He is a member of the American Psychological Association, New York State Psychological Association, National Association of School Psychologists, Suffolk County Psychological Association, Psi Chi, American Association of University Professors, and the Council for Exceptional Students.

Dr. Giuliani is the president of the National Association of Parents with Children in Special Education (NAPCSE), executive director of the National Association of Special Education Teachers (NASET), and executive director of the American Academy of Special Education Professionals (AASEP). He is a consultant for school districts and early childhood agencies and has provided numerous workshops for parents and guardians and teachers on a variety of special education and psychological topics. Dr. Giuliani is the coauthor of numerous books by Corwin Press, including *The Big Book of Special Education Resources* and the *Step-by-Step Guide for Educators* series.

1

Introduction to ASD

IDEA Definition of ASD

Under our nation's federal special education law, the Individuals with Disabilities Education Act 2004 (IDEA, 2004), all types of ASD are classified under one term, *autism*.

Under IDEA 2004, *autism* is defined as

> a developmental disability significantly affecting verbal and nonverbal communication and social interaction, usually evident before age 3, that adversely affects a child's educational performance. Other characteristics often associated with ASD are engagement in repetitive activities and stereotyped movements, resistance to environmental change or change in daily routines, and unusual responses to sensory experiences. The term does not apply if a child's educational performance is adversely affected because the child has an emotional disturbance. (300.8[c][1])

Important Point: Most practitioners and educators believe autism is a "spectrum" disorder; that is, a group of disorders with similar features, which can range from mild to severe. Throughout this book, we will refer to "autism" as "autism spectrum disorder" (ASD).

Overview of ASD

Originally described in 1943 by Leo Kanner (Colarusso & O'Rourke, 2004), ASD is an increasingly popular term that refers to a broad definition of ASD, including the classical form of the disorder as well as closely related disabilities that share many of the core characteristics.

ASD has many variations in symptoms or behavioral characteristics. Furthermore, people with ASD vary widely in abilities, intelligence, and behaviors across those indicators. That is, some or all of the characteristics associated with ASD may be observed in a range of mild to very severe forms. For example, some children do not speak; others have limited language. Those with more advanced language skills tend to use a small range of topics, as well as have difficulty with abstract concepts and pragmatic language skills. Repetitive play skills, a limited range of interests, and impaired social skills are generally evident as well. Unusual responses to sensory information, such as loud noises, lights, and certain textures or food or fabrics, are also common.

Individuals with ASD can exhibit severe mental retardation or be extremely gifted in their intellectual and academic accomplishments (Vaughn, Bos, & Schumm, 2003). While many individuals prefer isolation and tend to withdraw from social contact, others show high levels of affection and enjoyment in social situations. Some people with ASD appear lethargic and slow to respond, focusing more on objects than on other people (Scott, Clark, & Brady, 2000). Others are very active and seem to interact constantly with preferred aspects of their environment.

Causes of ASD

ASD is a neurological disability that is presumed to be present from birth and is always apparent before the age of three. Most researchers agree that the collection of symptoms constituting ASD arises from a set of inherited factors (Rodier, 2000). Although ASD affects the functioning of the brain, the specific cause of ASD is unknown. In fact, it is widely assumed that there are most likely multiple causes, each of which may be manifested in different forms, or subtypes, of ASD.

In the majority of cases, no specific underlying cause can be identified. However, a variety of factors are being investigated. These include infectious, metabolic, genetic, and environmental factors. Professionals generally agree that symptoms of ASD are triggered by malfunctions in the brain (Szatmari, Jones, Zwaigenbaum, & MacLean, 1998) and that trauma related to abuse or neglect by care-givers is not the cause (Gillberg & Coleman, 2000).

The search for physiological causes of ASD began in the 1960s (Scott et al., 2000). A working group convened by the National Institute of Health (NIH) in 1995 reached a consensus that ASD probably results from a genetic susceptibility that involves multi-ple genes. However, the research on chromosomal abnormalities in ASD shows no agreement as to what chromosome or chromosomes are implicated as a cause of ASD (International Molecular Genetics Study of Autism Consortium (IMGSAC), 1998; Konstantareas & Homatidis, 1999).

Some parents and families of children with ASD believe that the measles/mumps/rubella (MMR) vaccine caused their children's ASD. These parents report that their children were "normal" until they received the MMR vaccine. Then, after getting the vaccine, their children started showing symptoms of ASD. Because the symptoms of ASD began to occur around the same time as the child's MMR vaccination, parents and families see the vaccine as the cause of the ASD. However, just because the events happen around the same time does not mean that one caused the other. Although children receive many other vaccines in addition to the MMR vaccine, these other vaccines have not been identified as pos-sible causes of ASD.

These parents' beliefs and observations were reinforced by a small study of bowel disease and ASD published by Wakefield and his col-leagues in 1998 (Wakefield et al., 1998).The study's authors suggested that there was a link between the MMR vaccine and ASD. This study did not involve scientific testing to find out if there was a link. Rather, the authors relied on the reports of parents and families of 12 children with ASD to make their suggestion. The study did not provide scien-tific proof of any link.

Since this study was published in 1998, a number of other studies have been published that suggest a link between the MMR vaccine and ASD, but none provides scientific proof of such a link.

To date, there is no conclusive evidence that any vaccine increases the risk of developing ASD or any other behavior disorder. Currently, no study provides definitive evidence of an association between ASD and vaccines (Dales, Hammer, & Smith, 2001; Stratton, Gable, Shetty, & McCormick, 2001). However, continued research is needed to examine the mechanisms of ASD and any possible rela-tionship to vaccines.

Prevalence and Incidence of ASD

According to the *26th Annual Report* (U.S. Department of Education, 2004), 140,473 students between the ages of 6 to 21 were identified as having ASD. This represents approximately 2.3 percent of all students having a classification in special education and approximately 0.12 percent of all school-age students.

A controversial finding is that prevalence figures for ASD have increased dramatically over the past 30 to 40 years, leading some to claim that there is an "ASD epidemic." In the most recent government survey on the rate of ASD (2007 survey based on data from 2000 and 2002), the Centers for Disease Control and Prevention (CDC, 2007a) found a rate higher than that reported in studies conducted in the United States during the 1980s and early 1990s. The CDC survey assigned a diagnosis of ASD based on health and school records of 8-year-olds in 14 communities throughout the United States. Debate continues about whether this represents a true increase in the prevalence of ASD. Changes in the criteria used to diagnose ASD, along with increased recognition of the disorder by professionals and the public, may all be contributing factors. Nonetheless, the CDC report confirms other recent epidemiologic studies documenting that more children are being diagnosed with ASD than before.

Data from an earlier report of the CDC's Atlanta-based program found the rate of ASD was 3.4 per 1,000 for children 3–10 years of age. Summarizing this and several other major studies on ASD prevalence, CDC estimates that 2–6 per 1,000 (from 1 in 500 to 1 in 150) children have ASD. The risk is 3–4 times higher in males than females. Compared to the prevalence of other childhood conditions, this rate is lower than the rate of mental retardation (9.7 per 1,000 children) but higher than the rates for cerebral palsy (2.8 per 1,000 children), hearing loss (1.1 per 1,000 children), and vision impairment (0.9 per 1,000 children). The CDC notes that these studies do not provide a national estimate (CDC, 2007b).

Age of Onset of ASD

Symptoms of ASD usually appear during the first three years of childhood and continue throughout life (Friend, 2005). Interestingly, in close to 50 percent of children diagnosed with ASD, the defining characteristics do not become evident until the child is a toddler, at which point some of the children begin to regress markedly in communication and social abilities (Davidovitch, Glick, Holtzman, Tirosh, & Safir, 2000).

Gender Features of ASD

According to the American Psychiatric Association's *Diagnostic and Statistical Manual of Mental Disorders: Text Revision* (2000), the prevalence rate of ASD in males is about four times higher than in females. Other studies have found ratios as high (Kadesjo, Gillberg, & Hagberg, 1999) or higher (Scott, Baron-Cohen, Bolton, & Brayne, 2002). Although debate exists on this issue, it is clear that ASD is diagnosed much more often in males rather than females. When females do have ASD, however, they are more likely to have cognitive deficits (National Research Council, 2001, cited in Hallahan & Kauffman, 2006).

Cultural Features of ASD

ASD has been found throughout the world in people of all racial and social backgrounds. It exists at approximately the same level in all racial and ethnic groups and among individuals at all income levels (U.S. Department of Education, 2004).

Familial Pattern of ASD

Recent studies strongly suggest that some people have a genetic predisposition to ASD. Scientists estimate that, in families with one child with autism, the risk of having a second child with the disorder is approximately 5 percent, or 1 in 20, which is greater than the risk for the general population (Yirmiya, Shaked, & Erel, 2001).

Educational Implications of Students With ASD

The question as to whether a student with ASD should be fully included in the general education classroom is a subject of great controversy. Many studies support full inclusion (Kliewer & Biklen, 1996; Stainback & Stainback, 1990), while many others indicate the need for a full continuum of services (Klingner, Vaughn, Schumm, Cohen, &

Forgan, 1998; Padeliadu & Zigmond, 1996). Today, more than half the students (57 percent) with ASD receive services in a self-contained classroom or more restrictive environment; approximately 25 percent are assigned to the general education classroom (U.S. Department of Education, 2004).

Appropriate educational programs and determining a diagnosis early are critical to children with ASD. Students with ASD need educational curriculums and programs that focus on improving numerous types of skills. These include communication, social, academic, behavioral, and daily living skills (National Dissemination Center for Children with Disabilities, 2007).

Appropriate educational programs need to be designed for children with ASD to afford them the greatest possible opportunities for future transition to living and working in the community and secure paid employment in competitive settings (Bock & Myles, 1999; Bowe, 2005; Cowley, 2000).

Evidence-Based Practice in Working With Children With ASD and Their Families

The best way to help individuals with ASD involves a team effort, with parents playing an integral role as respected partners.

> No one individual or group of individuals has unlocked all of the complex variables involved in ASD. . . . A coordinated effort by all involved can greatly enhance the functioning level of the child with ASD and concomitantly reduce the tremendous familial stress associated with having a child with a disability. (Koegel & Koegel, 1995, pp. ix–x)

Parents need to be seen as collaborators in their child's treatment programs beginning at the time of diagnosis. As children age, they should also be increasingly involved in decision making in all aspects of their lives. Many individuals with ASD will need an interdisciplinary team that functions as a unit throughout their lives. "Given the intensity and unique pattern of stressors faced by families of children with ASD, the need for parent-professional collaboration in ASD intervention is paramount" (Volkmar, Paul, Klin, & Cohen, 2005, pp. 1059–1060).

The *Handbook of Autism and Pervasive Developmental Disorders* (Volkmar et al., 2005) cites eight research-based general approaches that are "most relevant to working with families of children with ASD" (p. 1061). These are defined as the following:

- Provide family members with information from the professional literature in an organized and accessible format.
- Train parents to implement instruction techniques or behavior management strategies.
- Help family members apply principles of learning to education and management.
- Work with family members to increase the positive valence and decrease the negative aspects of parent-child relationships.
- Train family members in cognitive techniques in order to modify emotional and behavioral responses.
- Provide family members with empathy, a listening ear, and basic problem solving either through individual sessions or group work.
- Assist family members in obtaining access to resources, services, and basic necessities.
- Assist family members in advocating for the identified child's needs across the lifetime. (pp. 1062–1063)

Research Basis for Services to Children With ASD in the Home, School, and Community

Children with ASD are a very heterogeneous group (ranging from toddlers who are nonverbal with significant developmental delays to young adults with above-average cognitive abilities but significant social and relating challenges) living and being educated in diverse circumstances. Therefore, it is unlikely that any one approach will work for all children with ASD in all circumstances. The complexity of ASD affects research into its causes and potential treatments. Different bodies of research address different aspects of service delivery to children with ASD and their families: different age groups; school versus home and community support; different diagnoses within the ASD spectrum; specific treatment, intervention, or educational strategies; and comprehensive program models. Also, different approaches are recommended for children and adolescents with Asperger syndrome. Recently, there has been considerable research regarding effectiveness of early intervention for young children with ASD. These bodies of research answer different questions regarding effectiveness (National Research Council, 2001).

There is much controversy in the field regarding appropriate treatment, support, and intervention for ASD. Many people have strongly held opinions regarding what is most appropriate and effective. Because the causes of ASD are unknown, the field has been particularly vulnerable to purported "cures" that do not stand up to scientific scrutiny. Each system has its own traditions and guiding philosophies regarding supporting children with disabilities. Some interventions may conflict with people's beliefs and philosophies.

There has been a recent push in both education and the social sciences to utilize evidence-based practices to maximize outcomes and cost-effectiveness. The federal No Child Left Behind Act promotes the use of scientifically based research to improve accountability and educational outcomes. Professional organizations, such as the American Psychological Association, are developing clinical practice guidelines that promote the use of evidence-based treatments. Evidence-based practices are those whose effectiveness is supported by high-quality, peer-reviewed research. No uniform standard exists in education or the social sciences for assessing the quality and quantity of research to determine that a given practice is evidence based. Instead, a variety of standards has been proposed by the professional and scientific communities (Pierangelo & Giuliani, 2007).

2

Characteristics of Children With ASD

While individuals with ASD can display a wide range of possible behaviors, some behaviors are commonly characteristic of the disorder. Familiarity with these is important as a basis of understanding their impact on educational programming. They include difficulties in the areas of social interaction, communication, sensory processing, and learning new skills. Not all of these characteristics will be present in all diagnosed cases, and they will vary for individual children at different ages. Also, characteristics commonly associated with ASD are not exclusive to ASD and could appear in individuals diagnosed with other disabilities.

Possible Early Indicators of ASD

Clinical clues, sometimes referred to as "red flags," are historical facts and current observations that, if present, increase concern about possible ASD in a young child. Clinical clues may be noticed by the parents, others familiar with the child, or a professional as part of routine development surveillance or during health care visits for some other reason.

The clinical clues listed in Table 2.1 represent delayed or abnormal behaviors that are seen in children with ASD (although some of these findings may also be seen in children who have a developmental delay or a disorder other than ASD).

Table 2.1   Clinical Clues of Possible ASD

- Delay or absence of spoken language
- Looks through people; not aware of others
- Not responsive to other people's facial expressions/feelings
- Lack of pretend play; little or no imagination
- Does not show typical interest in or play near peers purposefully
- Lack of turn taking
- Unable to share pleasure
- Qualitative impairment in nonverbal communication
- Does not point at an object to direct another person to look at it
- Lack of gaze monitoring
- Lack of initiation of activity or social play
- Unusual or repetitive hand and finger mannerisms
- Unusual reactions or lack of reaction to sensory stimuli

If clinical clues of possible ASD are identified by either parents or professionals, it is important to follow up with appropriate screening tests. For children with suspected ASD, it is important to do both a diagnostic evaluation (to determine the specific diagnosis) and a functional assessment (to evaluate the child's strengths and needs in various developmental domains).

Patterns of Development

Some children with ASD show hints of future problems within the first few months of life. In others, symptoms may not show up until 24 months or later. Studies have shown that one-third to one-half of parents of children with ASD notice a problem before their child's first birthday, and nearly 80–90 percent see problems by 24 months. Some children with ASD seem to develop normally until 18–24 months of age, and then they stop gaining new language and social skills or lose the skills they had.

Children with ASD develop at different rates in different areas of growth. They may have delays in language, social, and learning skills, while their motor skills are about the same as other children their age. They might be very good at putting puzzles together or solving computer problems, but they might have trouble with social activities like talking or making friends. Children with ASD might also learn a hard skill before they learn an easy one. For example, a child might be able to read long words but not be able to tell you what sound a *b* makes.

Impairments in Social Skills

Social impairments are one of the main problems in all people with ASD. These impairments are not merely social "difficulties" like shyness. They are bad enough to cause serious problems in everyday life. These social problems are often combined with the other areas of deficit, such as communication skills and unusual behaviors and interests. For instance, the inability to have a back-and-forth conversation is both a social and a communication problem.

Typical infants are very interested in the world and people around them. By the first birthday, a typical toddler tries to imitate words, uses simple gestures such as waving bye-bye, grasps fingers, and smiles at people. But the young child with ASD may have a very hard time learning to interact with other people. One way very young children interact with others is by imitating actions—for instance, clapping when mom claps. Children with ASD may not do this, and they may not show interest in social games like peek-a-boo or pat-a-cake. Although the ability to play pat-a-cake is not an important life skill, the ability to imitate is. We learn all the time by watching others and by doing what they do—especially in new situations and in the use of language.

People with ASD might not interact with others the way most people do. They might not be interested in other people at all. Some might want friends but have social problems that make those relationships difficult. They might not make eye contact and might just want to be alone. Many children with ASD have a very hard time learning to take turns and share—much more so than other children. This can make other children unwilling to play with them.

People with ASD may have problems with expression, so they might have trouble understanding other people's feelings or talking about their own feelings. Many people with ASD are very sensitive to being touched and might not want to be held or cuddled. Repetitive behaviors (called "self-stimulatory behaviors"), common among people with ASD, may seem odd to others or make them uncomfortable, causing them to shy away from a person with ASD.

Social issues, such as having trouble interacting with peers, saying whatever comes to mind even if it's inappropriate, adapting to change only with difficulty, and even poor grooming habits, can sometimes make it hard for adults with ASD to get and/or keep a job at their intellectual level. Anxiety and depression, which affect some people with ASD, can make existing social impairments even harder to manage.

Social skills that many people learn by watching others may need to be taught directly to people with ASD. When deciding what to teach, remember the social value of learning independent living skills such as toilet training and other basic grooming skills (bathing, tooth brushing, dressing appropriately, etc.).

Because children and adolescents with ASD are "different," and because they are often very literal and sometimes naïve and overly trusting, they are often the target of bullies and may be easily taken advantage of. It is very important to teach all children from a very young age to be tolerant and accepting of differences. It is also important to teach children and adolescents with ASD about personal safety and tell them to go to a parent, teacher, or other trusted adult if they need help.

There are many strategies and curriculum supplements for teaching children and adolescents with and without ASD about bullying and other personal safety issues. These can be found by visiting a local bookstore, searching an online bookseller, or by contacting a publishing company that specializes in disability-specific and/or education publications. Teachers and health care professionals are often good resources for this type of information as well.

Children with ASD also are slower in learning to interpret what others are thinking and feeling. Subtle social cues—whether a smile, a wink, or a grimace—may have little meaning. To a child who misses these cues, "Come here" always means the same thing, whether the speaker is smiling and extending her arms for a hug or frowning and planting her fists on her hips. Without the ability to interpret gestures and facial expressions, the social world may seem bewildering. To compound the problem, people with ASD have difficulty seeing things from another person's perspective. Most 5-year-olds understand that other people have different information, feelings, and goals than they have. A person with ASD may lack such understanding. This inability leaves them unable to predict or understand other people's actions.

Although not universal, it is common for people with ASD also to have difficulty regulating their emotions. This can take the form of "immature" behavior, such as crying in class or engaging in verbal outbursts that seem inappropriate to those around them. Individuals with ASD may also be disruptive and physically aggressive at times, making social relationships still more difficult. They have a tendency to "lose control," particularly in a strange or overwhelming environment or when angry and frustrated. They may at times break things, attack others, or hurt themselves. In their frustration, some bang their heads, pull their hair, or bite their arms.

Impairments in Communication Skills

Each person with ASD has different communication skills. Some people may have relatively good verbal skills, with only a slight language delay, along with impaired social skills. Others may not speak at all or have limited ability or interest in communicating and interacting with others. About 40 percent of children with ASD do not talk at all. Another 25–30 percent of children with ASD have some words at 12–18 months of age and then lose them. Others may speak, but not until later in childhood (Pierangelo & Giuliani, 2007).

People with ASD who do speak may use language in unusual ways. For example, they may not be able to combine words into meaningful sentences. Some people with ASD speak only single words, while others repeat the same phrases over and over. Some children repeat what others say, a condition called echolalia. The repeated words might be said right away or at a later time. For example, if you ask children with ASD, "Do you want some juice?" they might repeat, "Do you want some juice?" instead of answering your question. Although many children without ASD go through a stage where they repeat what they hear, it normally passes by age 3. Some people with ASD can speak well but may have a hard time listening to what other people say.

People with ASD may have a hard time using and understanding gestures, body language, or tone of voice. For example, people with ASD might not understand what it means to wave good-bye. Facial expressions, movements, and gestures may not match what they are saying. For instance, people with ASD might smile while saying something sad. They might say "I" when they mean "you," or vice versa. Their voices might sound flat, robotlike, or high pitched. People with ASD might stand too close to people with whom they are talking or might stick with one topic of conversation for too long. They might talk a lot about something they really like rather than have a back-and-forth conversation with someone. Some children with relatively good language skills speak like little adults, failing to pick up on the "kid-speak" that is common in their peers.

By age 3, most children have passed predictable milestones on the path to learning language; one of the earliest is babbling. By the first birthday, typical toddlers say words, turn when they hear their name, point when they want a toy, and when offered something distasteful, make it clear that the answer is no.

Some infants who later show signs of ASD coo and babble during the first few months of life, but they soon stop. Others may be delayed, developing language as late as ages 5 to 9. Some children may learn to use communication systems such as pictures or sign language. Some children diagnosed with ASD remain mute throughout their lives.

Some children only mildly affected may exhibit slight delays in language, or they may even seem to have precocious language and unusually large vocabularies but have great difficulty in sustaining a conversation. The give-and-take of normal conversation is hard for them, although they often carry on a monologue on a favorite subject, giving no one else an opportunity to comment. Another difficulty is often the inability to understand body language, tone of voice, or "phrases of speech." They might interpret the sarcastic expression "Oh, that's just great," as meaning it really is great.

It can be hard to understand what ASD children are saying, and their body language can be difficult to understand as well when facial expressions, movements, and gestures do not match what the child is saying or reflect his feelings. Without meaningful gestures or the language to ask for things, people with ASD are at a loss to let others know what they need. As a result, they may simply scream or grab what they want. Until they are taught better ways to express their needs, ASD children do whatever they can to get through to others. As people with ASD grow up, they can become increasingly aware of their difficulties in understanding others and in being understood. As a result they may become anxious or depressed.

Unusual and Repeated Behaviors and Routines

Unusual behaviors, such as repetitive motions, may make social interactions difficult. Repetitive motions can involve part of the body or the entire body or even an object or toy. For instance, people with ASD may spend a lot of time repeatedly flapping their arms or rocking from side to side. They might repeatedly turn a light on and off or spin the wheels of a toy car in front of their eyes. These types of activities are known as self-stimulation or "stimming."

People with ASD often thrive on routine. A change in the normal pattern of the day—like a stop on the way home from school—can be very upsetting or frustrating to people with ASD. They may "lose control" and have a meltdown or tantrum, especially if they're in a strange place.

Also, some people with ASD develop routines that might seem unusual or unnecessary. For example, they might try to look in every window they walk by or may always want to watch a video in its entirety—from the previews at the beginning through the credits at the end. Not being allowed to do these types of routines may cause severe frustration and tantrums.

Although children with ASD usually appear physically normal and have good muscle control, odd repetitive motions may set them apart from other children. These behaviors might be extreme and highly apparent, or they may be more subtle. Some children and older individuals spend a lot of time repeatedly flapping their arms or walking on their toes. Some suddenly freeze in position.

As children, they might spend hours lining up their cars and trains in a certain way, rather than using them for pretend play. If someone accidentally moves one of the toys, the child may be tremendously upset. ASD children need, and demand, absolute consistency in their environment. A slight change in any routine—in mealtimes, dressing, taking a bath, going to school at a certain time and by the same route—can be extremely disturbing. Perhaps order and sameness lend some stability in a world of confusion.

Repetitive behavior sometimes takes the form of a persistent, intense preoccupation. For example, the child might be obsessed with learning all about vacuum cleaners, train schedules, or lighthouses. Often there is great interest in numbers, symbols, or science topics.

Additional Disabilities and Comorbid Conditions With ASD

Sensory Problems

When children's perceptions are accurate, they can learn from what they see, feel, or hear. On the other hand, if sensory information is faulty, the child's experiences of the world can be confusing. Many ASD children are highly attuned or even painfully sensitive to certain sounds, textures, tastes, and smells. Some children find the feel of clothes touching their skin almost unbearable. Some sounds—a vacuum cleaner, a ringing telephone, a sudden storm, even the sound of waves lapping the shoreline—will cause these children to cover their ears and scream.

In ASD, the brain seems unable to balance the senses appropriately. Some ASD children are oblivious to extreme cold or pain. A child with ASD may fall and break an arm yet never cry. Other children may bash their heads against a wall and not wince, but a light touch may make them scream with alarm.

Mental Retardation

Many children with ASD have some degree of mental impairment. When tested, some areas of ability may be normal, while others may be especially weak. For example, a child with ASD may do well on the parts of the test that measure visual skills but earn low scores on the language subtests.

Seizures

One in four children with ASD develops seizures, often starting either in early childhood or adolescence. Seizures, caused by abnormal electrical activity in the brain, can produce a temporary loss of consciousness (a blackout), a body convulsion, unusual movements, or staring spells. Sometimes a contributing factor is a lack of sleep or a high fever. An electroencephalogram (EEG), which records the electric currents in the brain by means of electrodes applied to the scalp, can help confirm the seizure's presence.

In most cases, seizures can be controlled by a number of medicines called "anticonvulsants." The dosage of the medication is adjusted carefully to use the least possible amount of medication that will be effective.

Fragile X Syndrome

This disorder is the most common inherited form of mental retardation. It was so named because one part of the X chromosome has a defective piece that appears pinched and fragile when under a microscope. Fragile X syndrome affects about 2–5 percent of people with ASD. It is important to have a child with ASD checked for fragile X, especially if the parents are considering having another child. For an unknown reason, if a child with ASD also has fragile X, there is a 50 percent chance that boys born to the same parents will have fragile X syndrome. Other members of the family who may be contemplating having a child may also wish to be checked for fragile X syndrome.

Tuberous Sclerosis

Tuberous sclerosis is a rare genetic disorder that causes benign tumors to grow in the brain as well as in other vital organs. It has a consistently strong association with ASD. From 1–4 percent of people with ASD also have tuberous sclerosis.

Associated Features

People with ASD might have a range of other behaviors associated with the disorder. These include hyperactivity, short attention span, impulsivity, aggressiveness, self-injury, and temper tantrums. They may have unusual responses to touch, smell, sound, and other sensory input. For example, they may over- or underreact to pain or to a loud noise. They may have abnormal eating habits. For instance, some people with ASD limit their diet to only a few foods, and others may eat nonfood items like dirt or rocks (this is called pica). They may also have odd sleeping habits. People with ASD may seem to have abnormal moods or emotional reactions. They may laugh or cry at unusual times or show no emotional response at times you would expect one. They may not be afraid of dangerous things or fearful of harmless objects. People with ASD may also have gastrointestinal issues such as chronic constipation or diarrhea.

It is important to remember that children with ASD can get sick or injured just like children without ASD. Regular medical and dental exams should be part of a child's intervention plan. Often it is hard to tell if a child's behavior is related to the ASD or is caused by a separate health problem. For instance, head banging could be a symptom of ASD, or it could be a sign that the child is having headaches. In those cases, a careful physical exam is important.

3

Types of ASDs

Autistic Disorder (Classic Autism)

Autistic disorder (sometimes called "classic autism") is the most common condition in a group of developmental disorders known as the autism spectrum disorders (ASDs). Classic autism is characterized by impaired social interaction; problems with verbal and nonverbal communication; and unusual, repetitive, or severely limited activities and interests (National Institute of Neurological Disorders and Stroke, 2005a).

Three distinctive behaviors characterize children with classic autism: difficulties with social interaction, problems with verbal and nonverbal communication, and repetitive behaviors or narrow, obsessive interests. The behaviors can range in impact from mild to disabling. Other common symptoms of classic autism include the following (Deutsch-Smith, 2004; Gargiulio, 2004; Heward, 2006; Westling & Fox, 2004):

- Does not respond to normal teaching methods
- Does not respond to verbal cues
- Engages in sustained odd play
- Exhibits minimal or no eye contact
- Exhibits over- or undersensitivity to pain
- Exhibits physical overactivity or extreme underactivity
- Has difficulty expressing and receiving physical affection

- Has difficulty expressing needs; uses gestures or pointing instead of words
- Has difficulty relating to and mixing with others
- Has no real fear of danger
- Maintains inappropriate attachments to objects
- Motor skills are uneven
- Often exhibits tantrums
- Prefers to be alone; aloof manner
- Repetition of words or phrases in place of normal, responsive language
- Shows resistance to change
- Spins objects

There is no known single cause for autistic disorder, but it is generally accepted that it is caused by abnormalities in brain structure or function. Brain scans show differences in the shape and structure of the brain in children with autism versus those without autism. Researchers are investigating a number of theories, including the link between genetics and medical problems. In many families, there appears to be a pattern of ASD or related disabilities, further supporting a genetic basis of the disorder (National Institute of Neurological Disorders and Stroke, 2005a). While no one gene has been identified as causing ASD, researchers are searching for irregular segments of genetic code that children with ASD may have inherited. It also appears that some children are born with a susceptibility to ASD but develop the disorder in response to an environmental "trigger," which researchers have not yet identified.

Childhood Disintegrative Disorder

Childhood disintegrative disorder is a condition occurring in 3- and 4-year-olds who have developed normally to age 2. Over several months, a child with this disorder will deteriorate in intellectual, social, and language functioning from previously normal behavior (U.S. National Library of Medicine, 2004b).

Childhood disintegrative disorder develops in children who have previously seemed perfectly normal. Typically language, interest in the social environment, and often toileting and self-care abilities are lost, and there may be a general loss of interest in the environment. The child usually comes to look very "autistic" (i.e., the clinical presentation, but not the history, becomes typical of a child with ASD) (Yale Developmental Disabilities Clinic, 2005). An affected child shows a loss of communication skills, has regression in nonverbal behaviors, and suffers a significant loss of previously acquired life skills. The condition is very similar to classic autism.

Symptoms of childhood disintegrative disorder may include (U.S. National Library of Medicine, 2004b):

- Loss of social skills
- Loss of bowel and bladder control
- Loss of expressive or receptive language
- Loss of motor skills
- Lack of play
- Failure to develop peer relationships
- Impairment in nonverbal behaviors
- Delay or lack of spoken language
- Inability to start or sustain a conversation

Childhood disintegrative disorder must be differentiated from both childhood schizophrenia and pervasive developmental disorder (PDD). The most important signs of childhood disintegrative disorder are loss of developmental milestones (U.S. National Library of Medicine, 2004b). The child tends to have normal development through age 3 or 4 and then, over a few months, gradually loses previously established abilities listed above (e.g., language, motor, or social skills). The cause is unknown but has been linked to neurological problems (Yale Developmental Disabilities Clinic, 2005).

Rett Syndrome

Rett syndrome (RS) is a neurological disorder seen almost exclusively in females and found in a variety of racial and ethnic groups worldwide (International Rett Syndrome Foundation, 2005).

An inability to perform motor functions is perhaps the most severely disabling feature of Rett syndrome, interfering with every body movement, including eye gaze and speech. Other diagnostic symptoms of Rett syndrome include (International Rett Syndrome Foundation, 2005; National Institute of Neurological Disorders and Stroke, 2005c):

- An early period of apparently normal or near-normal development until 6–18 months
- A period of temporary stagnation or regression, during which the child loses communication skills and purposeful use of the hands

- Stereotyped hand movements
- Gait disturbances
- Slowing of the rate of head growth
- Seizures
- Disorganized breathing patterns that occur when awake
- Compulsive hand movements, such as wringing and washing, following the loss of functional use of the hands

Pervasive Developmental Disorder Not Otherwise Specified (PDD-NOS)

Pervasive developmental disorder not otherwise specified (PDD-NOS) is a developmental-neurologic spectrum disorder occurring in 10 to 12 of every 10,000 children. Children with PDD-NOS (a) do not fully meet the symptomatic criteria clinicians use to diagnose any of the four specific types of PDD listed above, and/or (b) do not have the degree of impairment described in any of the above PDD-specific types. PDD-NOS presents similarly to ASD (some people argue that these conditions should be combined as one), but the child will have a lesser degree of a severe impairment. These kids are more likely to be verbal and have some degree of verbal or nonverbal effective communication, yet they must have features of ASD and a severe impairment in social interaction, communication, or repetitive stereotype behavior. This term is reserved for children with a severe impairment who do not fully qualify for any other autistic diagnosis, whether due to age of onset or combination of autistic features.

Asperger Syndrome

In Asperger syndrome (AS), a young child experiences impaired social interactions and develops limited repetitive patterns of behavior (Nemours Foundation, 2005). Motor milestones may be delayed, and clumsiness is often observed (U.S. National Library of Medicine, 2004a). However, people with AS usually have fewer problems with language than those with ASD, often speaking fluently, although their words can sometimes sound formal or stilted. People with AS do not usually have the accompanying learning disabilities associated with ASD; in fact, people with AS are often of average or above-average intelligence (National Autistic Society, 2005).

School-age children with AS exhibit a range of characteristics with varying degrees of severity. Diagnostic symptoms of Asperger disorder include the following (Friend, 2005; Hallahan & Kauffman, 2006; Mayo Clinic, 2006; National Institute of Neurological Disorders and Stroke, 2005a; Turnbull, Turnbull, & Wehmeyer, 2006; U.S. National Library of Medicine, 2004a; Westling & Fox, 2004).

Social Skills

- Has difficulty making friends.
- Engages in one-sided, long-winded conversations, without noticing if the listener is listening or trying to change the subject.
- Displays unusual nonverbal communication, such as lack of eye contact, few facial expressions, or awkward body postures and gestures.
- Doesn't empathize with or seem sensitive to others' feelings and has a hard time "reading" other people or understanding humor.
- Doesn't understand the give-and-take of conversation or engage in small talk.
- Seems egocentric or self-absorbed.
- May speak in a voice that is monotone, rigid, jerky, or unusually fast.
- Can be extremely literal or have difficulty understanding the nuances of language, despite having a good vocabulary.

Behavior

- Shows an intense obsession with one or two specific, narrow subjects, such as baseball statistics, train schedules, weather, or snakes.
- Likes repetitive routines or rituals.
- May memorize information and facts easily, especially information related to a topic of interest.
- May have clumsy, uncoordinated movements; an odd posture; or a rigid gait.
- May perform repetitive movements, such as hand or finger flapping.
- May engage in violent outbursts, self-injurious behaviors, tantrums, or meltdowns.
- May be hypersensitive to sensory stimulation, such as light, sound, and texture.

Asperger syndrome is a neurobiological disorder named for a Viennese physician, Hans Asperger, who in 1944 published a paper that described a pattern of behaviors in several young boys who had normal intelligence and language development but who also exhibited autistic-like behaviors and marked deficiencies in social and communication skills (National Institute of Neurological Disorders and Stroke, 2005a).

Overall, people with AS are quite capable of functioning in everyday life, but they tend to be somewhat socially immature and may be seen by others as odd or eccentric (Nemours Foundation, 2005). They have higher intelligence and communication skills than those with classic or more severe forms of ASD, but they display most, if not all of the other characteristics of ASD, with their primary difficulties manifested in poor social interactions (Hallahan & Kauffman, 2006).

4

Eligibility Criteria for Children With ASD

Step 1: Review of the Characteristics of Children With ASD

The following are the most common signs and symptoms of a child with ASD:

- The child exhibits impairments in communication.
- The child exhibits impairments in social interaction.
- The child exhibits patterns of behavior, interests, and/or activities that are restricted, repetitive, or stereotypic.
- The child exhibits unusual responses to sensory information.

See Chapter 2, "Characteristics of Children With ASD," for specific details on each of these characteristics.

Step 2: Determination of the Procedures and Assessment Measures to Be Used

If a child is suspected of having ASD, the following procedures and assessment measures should be used:

- A developmental profile that describes the child's historical and current characteristics associated with ASD
  - o The evaluator must establish that the child had characteristics of ASD in early childhood. The developmental profile describes the child's historical and current characteristics associated with ASD in the following areas from the eligibility criteria:
    - Impairments in communication
    - Impairments in social interaction
    - Patterns of behavior, interests, and/or activities that are restricted, repetitive, or stereotypic
    - Unusual responses to sensory information
    - The information must also demonstrate that the characteristics are
      - inconsistent or discrepant from the child's development in other area(s); and
      - documented over time and/or intensity.
  - o Behaviors characteristic of children with ASD must be viewed relative to the child's developmental level. The developmental profile should be organized to list characteristics of ASD the individual child displays within each area required by the eligibility criteria.
- At least three observations of the child's behavior, one of which involves direct interactions with the child
  - o The observations shall occur in multiple environments, on at least two different days, and be completed by one or more licensed professionals knowledgeable about the behavioral characteristics of ASD.
  - o A minimum of three observations should be done because individuals with ASD may function differently under different conditions. Important environments to observe are unstructured periods (e.g., breaks, recess, lunch, free time, free play, at home), large-group instruction, and structured sessions. Observations during changes in routines, interactions in the home environment, and unfamiliar environments may also help to develop an accurate picture of the child.
- An assessment of communication to address the communication characteristics of ASD, which includes but is not limited to measures of language semantics and pragmatics completed by a speech and language pathologist
- A medical statement or a health assessment statement indicating whether any physical factors may be affecting the child's educational performance

o The school district will send (either directly or through the parent) the health assessment form to the student's physician or physician's assistant to determine if the team should consider any physical factors in determining the underlying causes of the child's behavior. The physician may indicate there are no factors or may name factors that are present, such as mental retardation or seizures. The physician's statement may even indicate a child has a medical diagnosis of ASD. The team needs to consider any factors expressed by the physician as it completes the eligibility process. This statement alone will *not* determine if the student meets eligibility criteria for ASD; rather, it gives the team needed information about issues to consider as it makes eligibility decisions.

- An assessment using an appropriate behavioral rating tool or an alternative assessment instrument that identifies characteristics associated with ASD

  o The tools identify characteristics associated with ASD. They are used to help determine if the individual child demonstrates characteristics of ASD. The score on a behavior rating tool alone does *not* determine eligibility for ASD. The score and related information gained from completing the tool provide valuable information to the team when making the eligibility determination. However, no one piece of information alone is used to determine eligibility.

Additional Evaluations or Assessments Necessary to Identify the Child's Educational Needs

Some questions the team may ask include these:

- What is reinforcing to the child?
- What does the child find aversive?
- What are the child's interest areas?

For young children, teams must identify skills needed to progress developmentally. The individualized family service plan (IFSP) reflects both the child's development and special education needs. Children with IFSPs receive specially designed educational activities in the areas of development in which they are delayed.

For school-age children, teams must identify skills needed to participate in the general curriculum. The individualized education program (IEP) team's determination of how each child's disability affects the child's involvement and progress in the general curriculum is a primary consideration in the development of that child's IEP. In assessing children with disabilities, school districts may use a variety of assessment techniques to determine the extent to which these children can be involved and progress in the general curriculum. These assessment techniques may include criterion-referenced tests, standard achievement tests, diagnostic tests, other tests, or any combination of the above. Thus, the IEP team for each child with a disability must make an individualized determination regarding how the child will be involved and progress in the general curriculum and what needs that result from the child's disability must be met to facilitate that participation.

Besides these assessment measures, if a student is suspected of having a speech and language impairment under the definition set forth in IDEA, the following assessment measures should also be considered:

- An observation by a team member other than the student's regular teacher of the student's academic performance in a regular classroom setting or, in the case of a child less than school age or out of school, an observation by a team member conducted in an age-appropriate environment
- A developmental history, if needed
- An assessment of intellectual ability
- Other assessments of the characteristics of speech and language impairments if the student exhibits impairments in any one or more of the following areas: cognition, fine motor, perceptual motor, communication, social or emotional, and perception or memory. These assessments shall be completed by specialists knowledgeable in the specific characteristics being assessed.
- A review of cumulative records, previous individualized education programs or individualized family service plans, and teacher-collected work samples
- If deemed necessary, a medical statement or health assessment statement indicating whether any physical factors may be affecting the student's educational performance
- Assessments to determine the impact of the suspected disability
  - o on the student's educational performance when the student is at the age of eligibility for kindergarten through age 21 and
  - o on the child's developmental progress when the child is age 3 through the age of eligibility for kindergarten
- Additional evaluations or assessments necessary to identify the student's educational needs

Step 3: Determination of Eligibility for a Diagnosis of ASD

ASD is defined as a clinical disorder. Clinical diagnosis is made by a professional with expertise in evaluating children with a variety of behavioral and emotional disorders, including ASD. Typically, such evaluations are conducted by child psychiatrists, clinical child psychologists, clinical neuropsychologists, and specially trained neurologists and developmental pediatricians. In addition, many professionals may administer brief screening tools or parental report rating scales designed to identify children who may be at risk of a pervasive developmental disorder or who may show early signs of the disorder.

> **Important Point**: The eligibility criteria for classifications under IDEA are not specifically stated under the law. Therefore, the eligibility criteria for a particular disability may differ from state to state. Therefore, the information pertaining to "eligibility" is the authors' professional interpretation based on reviewing the states' guidelines and criteria for ASD.

To receive the classification of ASD child with a disability for special education services under IDEA, criteria 1 through 7 should be met:

1. *The child exhibits impairments in communication.* The child is unable to use expressive and receptive language for social communication in a developmentally appropriate manner, lacks nonverbal communication skills or uses abnormal nonverbal communication, uses abnormal form or content when speaking, and/or is unable to initiate or sustain conversation with others.

2. *The child exhibits difficulties in forming appropriate relationships.* The child exhibits deficits relating to people, marked lack of awareness of others' feelings, abnormal seeking of comfort at times of distress, absent or abnormal social play, and/or inability to make friends. The child does not relate to or use objects in an age-appropriate or functional manner.

3. *The child exhibits unusual responses to sensory information.* The child exhibits unusual, repetitive, nonmeaningful responses to auditory, visual, olfactory, taste, tactile, and/or kinesthetic stimuli.

4. *The child exhibits impairments in cognitive development.* The child has difficulty with concrete versus abstract thinking, awareness, judgment, and/or the ability to generalize. The child may exhibit exceptionally repetitive thinking (called "perseverative thinking") or impaired ability to process symbolic information.

5. *The child exhibits an abnormal range of activities.* The child shows a restricted repertoire of activities, interests, and imaginative development evident through stereotyped body movements, persistent preoccupation with parts of objects, distress over trivial changes in the environment, unreasonable insistence on routines, restricted range of interests, or preoccupation with one narrow interest.

6. *The child has been previously diagnosed with ASD by a qualified professional.* A licensed clinical psychologist, psychiatrist, clinical neuropsychologist, specially trained neurologist, developmental pediatrician, or other specific medical or mental health professional qualified to diagnose ASD has previously diagnosed the child, and the diagnosis was accompanied by a report with recommendations for instruction.

7. *The disability (ASD) is adversely affecting the child's educational performance.* The IEP team uses multiple sources of information to determine that educational performance is adversely affected by ASD, not primarily by an emotional disability.

Final Thoughts on Eligibility

Various conditions may be mistaken for ASD and vice versa. ASD can also coexist with other disorders. It is important to consider carefully the conditions with which ASD may be confused:

- Mental retardation
- Attention deficit hyperactivity disorder (ADHD)
- Fetal alcohol syndrome
- Obsessive-compulsive disorder
- Tourette syndrome
- Emotional disturbance

Teams need to seek out the appropriate resources for help in distinguishing the characteristics of other developmental, behavioral, and medical conditions. Resources may include both educators and medical providers specializing in, and experienced with, the various conditions. Accurate differential diagnosis is essential to avoid misleading assumptions in remediation plans and prognosis for the future. Differential diagnosis requires experience with a wide range of childhood developmental disorders. The team is required to consider whether the student requires special education services; that is, specially designed instruction to meet the unique needs of the child.

5

Overview of Effective Interventions

There is still considerable debate in the field regarding the most effective interventions for children with ASD. A variety of models and intervention strategies are being promoted as effective interventions. They range from applied behavior analysis to relationship-based models and specific skill-based intervention to physiologically oriented interventions. This chapter does not present a complete list of all interventions used but gives an overview of some of the most frequently cited, as well as the research regarding their effectiveness.

Behavioral Approaches

Applied Behavior Analysis (ABA)

ABA, a systematic approach for increasing desired behaviors and decreasing undesired behaviors, is grounded upon the principles of learning theory. Specifically, it is based upon the premise that behavior is influenced by environmental events. This understanding leads to structured interventions focused on measurable units of behavior. Data is gathered regularly for the purposes of assessment, monitoring of progress, and guiding adjustments in intervention. ABA has a significant research base, which supports its effectiveness in addressing a wide range of behaviors and skills for individuals with disabilities, including ASD.

A variety of national model programs for children with ASD are based on an ABA framework. Research supports the positive gains from these approaches and models in various areas such as social skills, communication, and measured IQ. Because of differences in approaches and model programs based on ABA, however, general statements cannot be made about the effectiveness of ABA as a treatment for ASD. The research does support specific gains for specific interventions. However, while many children have made significant progress with interventions and model programs based upon ABA, not all children have benefited to the same degree and not in the same areas of functioning. The research cannot tell us at this point which interventions will work for which children. Despite these limitations in the current research, ABA has strong empirical support for its effectiveness for addressing a wide range of areas affected by ASD (Herbert, Sharp, & Gaudiano, 2002; National Research Council, 2001; Simpson, 2005).

Discrete Trial Training

Discrete trial training is one method within the ABA framework of teaching new skills. Each trial includes the presentation of a stimulus or teacher's instruction, the child's response, and the consequence. The consequence is based upon whether the child's response was correct or not. A correct response is reinforced with praise or a tangible reinforcer, while incorrect responses result in correction such as verbal feedback or physical guidance. This type of training generally includes multiple trials teaching a specific behavior.

Discrete trial training has been effective in initially teaching a variety of skills. However, skills need to be expanded quickly to more natural environments to promote generalization. In this teacher-directed approach, the adult initiates the activity, determines the expected response, and provides the reinforcement (Prizant & Wetherby, 1998). Support for discrete trial training comes from the Young ASD Program at the University of California–Los Angeles, initiated by O. Ivar Lovaas in 1970.

Pivotal Response Training (PRT)

PRT involves teaching pivotal behaviors, or those central to a child's day-to-day functioning (e.g., motivation, responsiveness to multiple cues, self-initiation, empathy, self-regulation, social interaction) with the ultimate goal of facilitating generalized improvements across contexts. The premise is that teaching pivotal behaviors should result in widespread positive effects on many other behaviors. PRT includes providing opportunities for a child to respond spontaneously to a clear question or instruction; interspersing maintenance tasks (those the child can do) with novel tasks (those the child will be learning); sharing control, or giving the child choice in selecting a learning task; and structuring the environment so that the child can respond to multiple cues. It also involves use of natural consequences and reinforcers.

This approach uses a behavioral approach to teaching in natural contexts, building on the interests and motivations of the child with ASD. A comprehensive review of the research on PRT (Humphries, 2003) concluded that "the evidence supports claims that PRT is effective in improving the social-emotional and communicative behavior of young children with ASD. Therefore PRT is recommended as an evidence-based intervention for this purpose" (p. 5). PRT is a promising practice for increasing skills in a variety of areas affected by ASD.

Relationship-Based Models

Developmental, Individual Differences (DIR)

Another frequently promoted approach is DIR (also known as relationship-based therapy or floortime), developed in the early 1980s by Stanley Greenspan and Serena Weider. DIR is a developmentally based intervention based upon the premise that early learning grows out of intimate relationships with caregivers. The strategy involves starting where the child is at developmentally and building up skills by promoting and elaborating on communication interactions between the child and caregiver. The caregiver follows the lead of the child in a play situation and gradually encourages longer and more complex interactions.

Support for this model of intervention is based on testimonials and a chart review of 200 children completed retrospectively by Greenspan and Wieder (1997). They found that 58 percent of the children were deemed to have "very good outcomes," including purposeful organized problem-solving interactions, increased trust and intimate connections with parents, displaying more pleasurable affect, and heightened capacity for abstract thinking. The research for

DIR is not based upon experimental design but was a retrospective chart review published in a non-peer-reviewed journal founded by the authors. A recent study on the use of a developmental, social-pragmatic language intervention, which incorporated many of the components of DIR, showed an increase in spontaneous language for two of three young children with ASD (Ingersoll, Dvortcsak, Whalen, & Sikora, 2005). This well-designed study provides some preliminary support for this intervention to increase language. Additional research is needed to verify the effectiveness of this approach. DIR is a possibly efficacious intervention.

Relationship Development Intervention (RDI)

RDI is a parent-based program developed to target deficits in "experience sharing" in a systematic manner, resembling stages of typical development. After an initial evaluation of the child's functioning, parents receive several days' training from an RDI consultant. Training focuses on building motivation, modifying the communication style, enhancing memory formation, developing user-friendly practice environments, and generalizing motivation and skills into everyday life. Through the use of videotapes of home sessions and live consultation, parents receive feedback and ongoing training. Later, the strategies are used with an individual peer and in small groups.

Skills-Based Interventions

Social Stories

Social stories are short stories that describe a social situation and provide information about relevant social cues (e.g., what they mean and why they occur) to help an individual reflect on appropriate responses (Gray, 1995). They have been reported as effective for preschoolers through adults and particularly for those who have an interest in written or literacy-based material (Swaggart et al., 1995). They are used to teach social skills and appropriate behavior for particular situations. Research indicates fewer inappropriate social behaviors for children with ASD in the home and school settings following the use of social stories (Cullain, 2000; Kuoch & Mirenda, 2003; Kuttler, Myers, & Carlson, 1998; Norris & Dattilo, 1999; Swaggart et al., 1995). Social stories are a promising practice.

Video Modeling

Video modeling is a visual strategy that clarifies the roles and responsibilities people take on in particular situations or how to perform a specific skill. People with ASD watch short videos of adults, peers, or themselves performing an identified skill or task. Then they are provided opportunities to practice those skills in their daily lives. Video modeling has been used to teach skills such as greeting, naming or labeling, independent play, cooperative and social play, self-help skills (Charlop-Christy, Le, & Freeman, 2000), responding to questions and asking questions, and participating in a back-and-forth conversational exchange around a specified topic (Charlop & Milstein, 1989). It has also been applied to teach daily living skills such as pet care, table setting, and making orange juice (Shipley-Benamou, Lutzker, & Taubman, 2002). Video modeling has also been effective in teaching children to take the perspective of another person (Charlop-Christy & Daneshvar, 2003; LeBlanc et al., 2003). A review of the research on video modeling for children with ASD found 15 studies on this topic, with all but one showing positive results (Ayers & Langone, 2005). Their conclusion was that video modeling is a promising tool for teaching social and functional life skills.

Facilitated Communication

Facilitated communication (FC) is a method of supporting individuals with severe communication problems while they type messages. It involves providing physical and emotional support to the person typing. Considerable controversy surrounded this intervention, as the authorship of the communication was questioned given the level of physical support provided to the communicator. The use of FC has been rejected by much, but not all, of the scientific and professional community (American Academy of Pediatrics, 1998; Herbert et al., 2002; Perry & Condillac, 2003; Simpson, 2005).

There are over 50 research studies of FC with 143 communicators. The American Speech-Language-Hearing Association (1994) has stated that there is a lack of scientific evidence validating FC skills and a preponderance of evidence of facilitator influence on messages attributed to communicators. (ASHA Technical Report, 1994, in National Research Council, 2001, p. 62)

Additional problems arose when parents or caregivers were accused of abuse by people using FC.

However, "while the research studies do not support the validity of this intervention, there have been some qualitative studies indicating that some children with ASD have learned independent communication skills through FC" (Beukelman & Mirenda, 1998, cited in National Research Council, 2001, p. 62). They further suggest that the lack of validation of FC should not dissuade teams from considering training in the use of augmentative and alternative communication systems, including the use of keyboards. However, the goal must be independent use of the system without physical support, and communication prior to independence should be viewed with skepticism and need for validation.

A significant amount of research indicates that FC is not a valid method of communication, although some studies have shown that a few individuals have learned independent communication through FC (Weiss, Wagner, & Bauman, 1996). While a limited number of organizations support the use of FC, most professional organizations do not.

Structured Teaching: TEACCH

Structured teaching is an intervention philosophy developed by the University of North Carolina, Division TEACCH (Treatment and Education of Autistic and related Communication-handicapped CHildren). It allows for implementation of a variety of instructional methods (e.g., visual support strategies, picture exchange communication system (PECS), sensory integration strategies, discrete trial, music/rhythm intervention strategies, Greenspan's floortime, etc.). The following information outlines some important considerations for structured teaching to occur.

Eric Schopler, founder of Division TEACCH in the early 1970s, established the foundation for structured teaching in his doctoral dissertation by demonstrating that people with ASD process visual information more easily than verbal information (Schopler & Reichler, 1971).

What Is Structured Teaching?

- Structured teaching is based upon an understanding of the unique features and characteristics associated with the nature of ASD.
- Structured teaching describes the conditions under which a person should be taught rather than "where" or "what" (i.e., "learning how to learn").

- Structured teaching is a system for organizing students' environments, developing appropriate activities, and helping people with ASD understand what is expected of them.
- Structured teaching utilizes visual cues that help children with ASD focus on relevant information, which can at times be difficult for the person with ASD to distinguish from nonrelevant information.
- Structured teaching addresses challenging behaviors in a proactive manner by creating appropriate and meaningful environments that reduce the stress, anxiety, and frustration that children with ASD may experience.
- Structured teaching greatly increases a child's independent functioning (i.e., without adult prompting or cueing), which will assist him throughout life.

Primary Components of Structured Teaching

Physical Structure

Physical structure refers to the way in which we set up and organize the student's physical environment. It emphasizes where/how we place the furniture and materials invarious environments, including classrooms, playground, workshop/work area, bedroom, hallways, locker/cubby areas, etc.

Close attention to physical structure is essential for a number of reasons:

- Physical structure provides environmental organization for people with ASD.
- Clear physical and visual boundaries help the person to understand where each area begins and ends.
- The physical structure minimizes visual and auditory distractions.

The amount of physical structure needed depends on the level of self-control demonstrated by children, not their cognitive functioning level. As students learn to function more independently, the physical structure can be gradually lessened.

> **Example:** High-functioning children with ASD may display limited self-control. They will need a more highly structured environment than lower-functioning children displaying better self-control.

Physical structure consists of a number of components:

Location. Physical structure should be considered in any environment in which the person with ASD interacts.

Design/Layout. To establish clear visual and physical boundaries, each area of the classroom (or environment) should be clearly visually defined through the arrangement of furniture (e.g., bookcases, room dividers, office panels, shelving units, file cabinets, tables, rugs, etc.) and use of boundary markers, such as carpet squares or colored floor tape. Children with ASD typically do not automatically segment their environments as do typically developing children. In large, wide-open areas, children with ASD can have great difficulty understanding

- what is to occur in each area;
- where each area begins and ends; and
- how to get to a specific area by the most direct route.

Strategically placing furniture to define specific areas in clear visual terms will decrease the child's tendency to randomly wander/run from area to area. Visual physical boundaries can also be further defined within a specific area.

> **Example:** During group story time, a carpet square or taped-off square can provide children with ASD clear visual cues as to the physical boundaries of that activity. Floor tape can also be used in gym class to indicate to the children the area in which they should stay to perform certain motor skills, like warm-up exercises.
>
> **Example:** Color-coded placements (according to each child's assigned color) can be used for snack or mealtimes. The placements will visually and physically define each child's space (and food items) on the table.

These visual cues will help children with ASD better understand their environment, as well as increase their ability to become more independent in their environment and less reliant on an adult for direction.

Minimize Visual and Auditory Distractions. Visual distractions can be minimized with the following techniques:

- Painting the entire environment (walls, ceilings, bulletin boards, etc.) a muted color (e.g., off-white)
- Limiting the amount of visual "clutter," present in most classrooms in the form of art projects, seasonal decorations, and classroom materials
- Placing sheets/curtains to cover shelves of classroom materials, as well as other visually distracting equipment (e.g., computer, copy machine, TV/VCR, etc.)
- Storing unnecessary equipment/materials in another area

> **Example:** In the play area, limit the number of appropriate toys that the children can use and then, on a weekly basis, rotate in "new" toys while putting away the "old" ones.

- Using natural lighting from windows to reduce visually distracting fluorescent lighting
- Controlling the amount of light through the use of blinds, curtains, or shades, thus creating a warm and calm environment
- Placing study carrels and individual student work areas, bordered by a wall or corner of the classroom, away from group work tables to reduce environmental visual distractions
- Carefully considering where the child with ASD will sit in the regular education classroom

> **Example:** Tony, a student with ASD, was seated in the front of the class, facing away from the door and windows and away from shelves with instructional materials, to minimize visual distractions.

Auditory distractions can be reduced through the use of carpeting, lowered ceilings, and acoustical tiles; turning off the public-address system (or covering it with foam to mute the sound); and using headphones for appropriate equipment, such as the computer or tape players.

Develop Appropriate Instructional, Independent, Recreation, and Leisure Areas in Each Physically Structured Environment.
In a classroom setting, these areas may include the following:

- Small-group work area
- Independent work area
- 1:1 work area
- Play/recreation/leisure area
- Sensory motor area
- Crash/quiet area

At home, these areas may include the following:

- Independent work area
- Play area
- Crash/quiet area

Again, these specific areas should have clear visual boundaries to define each area for the child with ASD. It is also important to keep in mind the various distractions that may be present in each area, and make accommodations accordingly.

Organization. A physically structured environment must be extremely organized to effectively implement a structured teaching approach. Adequate storage of various materials (not in view of the students), which can also be easily accessed by the adults in the environment, is critical.

> **Example:** A sectioned-off storage area (with high dividing units to keep materials out of sight of the students) **within** the classroom can be very helpful to keep the environment "clutter and distraction-free" yet provide easy access to needed materials.

Students with ASD can also be taught to keep the physical environment structured and organized through the use of pictures, color-coding, numbers, symbols, etc.

> **Example:** In the play area, pictures of the toys can be placed on the shelves to provide structure when putting things away.

Visual Schedules

A daily visual schedule is a critical component in a structured environment. A visual schedule will tell the student with ASD what activities will occur and in what sequence.

Visual schedules are important for children with ASD because they do the following:

- Help address the children's difficulty with sequential memory and organization of time.
- Assist children with language comprehension problems to understand what is expected of them.
- Lessen the anxiety level of children with ASD and, thus, reduce the possible occurrence of challenging behaviors by providing the structure needed for students to organize and predict daily and weekly events. Schedules clarify that activities happen within a specific time period (e.g., understanding that "break time" is coming, but after "work time") and alert the students to any changes that might occur.
- Assist students in transitioning independently between activities and environments by telling them where to go next. Visual schedules can be used in all environments (e.g., classroom, gym, occupational therapy, speech/language therapy, home, Sunday school, etc.).
- Are based on a "first-then" strategy (i.e., "first you do ___, then you do ___,") rather than an "if-then" approach (i.e., "if you do ___, then you can do ___"). This first-then strategy allows the "first" expectation (whether a task, activity, or assignment) to be modified as needed. The modification is in terms of task completion and amount of prompting to accommodate the students' daily fluctuations in their ability to process incoming information. Then they can move on to their next visually scheduled tasks/activities.

Example: A student is having particular difficulty completing a math worksheet due to anxiety, sensory processing difficulties, communication, difficulty generalizing, internal/external distractions, change, etc. The assignment can be modified so that the child only has to complete three math problems *first,* and *then* the student has a sensory break, as indicated on his or her visual schedule.

- Can incorporate various social interactions into the student's daily schedule (e.g., showing completed work to a teacher/parent for social reinforcement, requiring appropriate social greetings).

- Can increase a student's motivation to complete less-enjoyable activities by strategically alternating more-preferred with less-preferred activities on the student's individual visual schedule.

> **Example:** By placing a computer time after math time, the student may be more motivated to complete math knowing that computer time will be next.

A visual schedule for a student with ASD must be directly taught and consistently used. Visual schedules should not be considered as "crutches" for students with ASD, from which they should gradually be "weaned." Instead, these individual visual schedules should be considered as "prosthetic" or "assistive tech" devices. For the student with ASD, the consistent use of a visual schedule is an extremely important skill. It has the potential to increase independent functioning throughout his life—at school, at home, and in the community.

Developing Visual Schedules. In general, schedules should be arranged in a top-to-bottom or left-to-right format, including a method for the student to manipulate the schedule to indicate that an activity is finished or "all done."

> **Examples:** Cross/mark off a finished activity with a dry-erase marker, place the item in an "all done" envelope/box, check off the item, draw a line through it, etc.

A minimum of two scheduled items should be presented at a time so that the student begins to understand that events and activities happen in a sequential manner, not in isolation.

Schedules can be designed using a variety of formats, depending upon the needs of the individual student.

> **Examples:** Object schedule, three-ring binder schedule, clipboard schedule, manila file folder schedules, dry-erase board schedules, Velcro strip across the top of the desk, etc.

Various visual representation systems can be used for an individual visual schedule, including the following:

- Real objects
- Photographs (e.g., Picture This software program or own photos)
- Realistic drawings
- Commercial picture system (e.g., Boardmaker software program)
- Written words/lists

Individual Schedule. It is necessary to develop an individual schedule for the child with ASD in addition to the general classroom schedule.

- An individual schedule will give the child with ASD important information in a visual form that the student can readily understand.
- Another consideration when individualizing a schedule for a student with ASD is the length of the schedule (number of activities). The length of the schedule may need to be modified due to the student's becoming increasingly obsessed and/or anxious regarding an upcoming scheduled activity or due to the student's difficulty in processing "too much" information presented at once.

> **Example:** A particular student "obsesses" over recess. If at the beginning of the day, the student sees "recess" scheduled later in the morning, he or she will continue to be obsessed with "going out for recess," resulting in increased anxiety and distractibility for all morning activities until recess. The student's schedule could be created with a few activity items at a time, up until recess. Again, individualization is the key to success.

- Some students may need a "check schedule" visual physical prompt to teach them to check their schedule independently, as well as learn the importance of their schedule.

> **Example:** "Check schedule" visual prompts can be made by writing the student's name on laminated colored paper strips or using popsicle sticks or poker chips with a large check printed on the chip, etc.

Transitions. Some students may need to transition to the next scheduled activity by taking their scheduled item (card or object) off their individual schedules and carrying it with them to the next activity/location. This may be due to the child's increased distractibility in maneuvering through the environment. The distractibility, or inability to sustain attention throughout the transition, is independent of the child's cognitive functioning level or verbal skills.

Example: Some nonverbal students with ASD, who function at a younger cognitive level, do not require transition schedule cards to get to the next scheduled activity. On the other hand, certain higher-functioning students with ASD require a transition card to get to the next scheduled activity due to their increased distractibility.

Teaching Components

Teaching components include work systems and visual structure.

Work Systems

Work systems are the systematic and organized presentation of tasks/materials so that students can learn to work independently, without adult directions/prompts. It is important to note that work systems can reflect any type of task(s) or activities (e.g., academic, daily living skills, recreation and leisure, etc.). Each work system, regardless of the nature of the specific task or activity, should address the following four questions:

1. *What is the work to be done? What is the nature of the task?* Examples: sorting by colors, adding/subtracting two-digit numbers, making a sandwich, brushing teeth, etc.

2. *How much work is to be done?* Visually represent to the students exactly how much work is to be done. If they are to cut out only ten soup can labels, don't give them a whole stack and expect them to count independently and/or understand that they are to cut out only ten labels for the task to be considered complete. Seeing the whole stack of labels—even if told that they should cut only ten—can cause children with ASD a great deal of frustration and anxiety in not being able to understand exactly how much work to complete.

   Remember, students with ASD rely upon their visual channel to process information; therefore, seeing a whole stack of work to complete can prove overwhelming. Provide only the materials the student will need for the specific task/activity to decrease possible confusion in understanding exactly how much and what work is to be done.

3. *When am I finished?* The students need to recognize independently when they are finished with a task/activity. The task itself may define this, or the use of timers or visual cues, such as a red dot to indicate where to stop on a particular worksheet, has proven effective.

4. *What comes next?* Items such as physical reinforcers, highly desired activities, break times, or free choice are highly motivating toward task completion. In some cases, simply being "all done" with the task motivates the child enough to complete it.

Experience with structured teaching and the use of work systems has shown that a student's overall productivity increases when the student has a way of knowing how much work there is to do, as well as when it is to be finished. Use of a work system helps to organize the child with ASD through use of a structured and systematic approach to completing various tasks independently.

Visual Structure

Visual structure is the process of incorporating concrete visual cues into the task/activity itself so that the students will not have to rely on the teacher's verbal or physical prompts to understand what to do. The students can use their strong visual skills to get meaning from the task/activity without adult assistance. Thus, these visual cues increase the students' ability to work successfully and independently.

Students with ASD tend to have difficulty processing the most obvious information in their environments, and at times, they may become overly focused or attentive to insignificant or irrelevant details. To help students with ASD identify and focus on the significant and relevant details of a task/activity, their daily activities/tasks need to be modified to incorporate visual instructions. A student should be able to sequentially complete a task/activity by looking at the visual instructions given. Visual instructions help the student to combine and organize a series of steps to obtain a desired outcome.

Through the use of a visually structured teaching method, a student with ASD can learn to complete various tasks/activities independently (i.e., without an adult's physical or verbal prompt). Therefore, many students with ASD can engage in independent work sessions for various periods throughout their day in any environment (home, school, work) and using any skill area (academic/curricular, daily living skills, recreation and leisure, etc.).

Conclusion

In conclusion, the structured teaching approach allows the student with ASD to learn a process of focusing upon and following visual cues in various situations and environments to increase overall independent functioning.

Physiologically Based Interventions

Sensory Integration

There is a consensus in the research that individuals with ASD often process sensory information differently than those without ASD. Some of these differences include either seeking out or having an aversion to sounds, touch, movements, oral sensations, pressure, and sight.

Sensory integration therapy involves providing sensory experiences that are designed to help the nervous system modulate, organize, and integrate information from the environment. This approach is supposed to allow for more adaptive responses to the environment. Reviews of existing research on the efficacy of sensory integration indicate that only limited research with small samples and uncontrolled designs has been done. Due to these limitations in the research, definitive conclusions cannot be drawn at this point; additional research is needed (Baranek, 2002; Dawson & Watling, 2000; Herbert et al., 2000; National Research Council, 2001; Perry & Condillac, 2003).

It is recommended that in designing supports, individuals with ASD be supported with strategies to cope with unusual sensory responses and/or that environments be modified to accommodate their sensitivities. In the absence of clear support for sensory integration, teams should identify expected outcomes from the intervention and use data to measure whether it is achieving the desired results. Sensory integration is currently an unsupported intervention.

Biological Interventions

There has been considerable use of complementary and alternative medicine for children with ASD. Some of the interventions being used include chelation therapy, craniosacral therapy, vitamin therapy, casein-free and gluten-free diets, secretin therapy, immunotherapy, antifungal medicines, and others. To date, the underlying physiological causes of ASD are unknown. There is not sufficient evidence to suggest that any of these alternative medicine approaches are effective, and some can have negative side effects (Herbert et al., 2002; Perry & Condillac, 2003). These interventions are either untested or unsupported.

Medication

Some psychotropic medications have been prescribed for children with ASD. They are not a cure for ASD but may help diminish some of the symptoms of ASD, such as anxiety and aggression. There is evidence that some of these medications, such as Risperdal (risperidone), are helpful (McDougle et al., 2000, in Volkmar et al., 2005). Because of their potential side effects, psychotropic medications should be used with caution and only as an adjunct to other educational and therapeutic approaches (Herbert et al., 2003; Volkmar et al., 2005).

Conclusion

In conclusion, there is strong support for intensive early intervention for preschool age children with ASD. While there are still questions regarding the most appropriate interventions, the strongest scientific support is for programs based upon ABA. Other interventions, such as DIR and RDI, show some promise but do not yet have sufficient evidence to support their efficacy. Research also shows more modest gains when interventions are started after preschool (Handleman & Harris, 2000). If intensive early intervention results in half of children with ASD functioning at a near typical level, in addition to the obvious benefits for the children and their families, the savings to the state in special education and human services costs over the lifetimes of these children would be substantial.

6

Creating Quality Educational Programs for Children With ASD

The importance of individualizing education programs for children with ASD and the importance of family involvement in those educational programs cannot be overstated. Programs will differ from child to child because of the uniqueness of ASD and the range of potential symptoms involved. There is consensus among researchers, practitioners, and educators that effective intervention begins early, usually by 30 months or earlier. Further, researchers and professionals have identified a number of strategies that are essential to implementing an effective program. The following are ten indicators in a quality educational program for children with ASD:

1. Family involvement

2. Comprehensive assessment of skills and deficits

3. Plan development/clearly defined goals and objectives

4. Effective teaching strategies

5. Assessment of the intervention

6. Structuring the environment

7. Applying functional behavior assessment to problem behavior

8. Transition

9. Opportunities with peers

10. Comprehensive team approach

1. Family Involvement

Parent and family involvement is an essential component of the educational program for a student with ASD. It is important for professionals and parents to agree about how often and in what format ongoing communication can best take place. Although frustrations are often inevitable, it is important for staff and parents to keep communication as positive and free of blame as possible. Professionals need to present information in a clear fashion, avoiding the use of educational or medical terminology that can be intimidating and confusing to family members. Problems experienced by family or school members should be discussed as soon as they arise and before they get out of control. To accomplish this task, teachers should involve parents in problem solving, and parents should not be afraid to ask questions about any aspect of their child's program.

2. Comprehensive Assessment of Skills and Deficits

A comprehensive assessment of a student's skills and abilities is the cornerstone of a quality individualized family service plan (IFSP) for children under 3 and an individualized education program (IEP) for children/students ages 3 to 21. By accurately determining the student's skill, strength, and deficit levels, appropriate goals and objectives can be written and accurate baselines determined.

Assessments may differ because of each child's/student's age and ability level. However, it is essential to consider the characteristics of ASD in completing each assessment. Thus, in addition to assessment of preacademic and academic skills, the assessment may also include prevocational and vocational skills, self-help and adaptive skills, communication, socialization, sensory regulation, motivation and reinforcement, behavior, fine and gross motor skills, play and leisure behaviors, as well as cognition.

Methods of assessment will be dependent upon individual student needs and ability level. It is important to realize that assessment is an ongoing process. For each child, a formalized assessment of skills must be conducted at regular intervals. The ongoing assessment results are then utilized to develop and change, as needed, the IFSP or IEP.

3. Plan Development/Clearly Defined Goals and Objectives

The key to teaching new skills, or improving emerging skills, is creating clearly defined IFSP outcomes or IEP goals and objectives that are developmentally appropriate; functional; and based on the assessment results, the student's strengths and interests, and the distinctive characteristics of ASD. Clearly, a number of factors must be considered in developing the individualized goals and objectives for students with ASD. Although individual goals will vary for each child based on age, diagnosis, and ability level, research has revealed that effective educational programs for students with ASD include goals addressing communication, social development, cognitive development, problem behaviors, sensory and motor development, and adaptive behavior.

In writing clearly defined outcomes or goals and objectives, Helfin and Simpson (1998) suggest the IFSP or IEP team should ask the following:

- Have meaningful outcomes been identified for the student?
- Were family members involved in identifying goals to be reinforced at home and school?
- Are the outcomes developmentally significant?
- Are the outcomes developmentally appropriate for the child?
- Have the characteristics of ASD been considered?
- Do the goals promote educational gain or merely address the symptoms of the disorder?
- Do the goals allow for generalization and maintenance of the newly acquired skills?

A review of goals and objectives would not be complete without a discussion of the importance of programming for the generalization and maintenance of newly acquired skills. *Generalization* is the ability to demonstrate a learned behavior or skill in a new or novel way, setting, environment, time, or date or among different individuals and materials. *Maintenance*, on the other hand, is the ability to demonstrate a skill over time. The ability to generalize and maintain meaningful skills that can be practiced and utilized within as well as outside of the classroom is essential to the success of each student's program. Meaningful tasks enhance the student's independence, give more opportunity for personal choice, and allow for more freedom in the community. Thus, the classroom teacher needs to work closely with the student's family as well as the support staff to ensure that new skills and desired behaviors can be practiced and reinforced in all settings: at home, at school, and in the community.

4. Effective Teaching Strategies

The following section provides practical, low-tech strategies for teaching students with ASD as well as a list of helpful resources. When choosing an intervention or teaching strategy, remember that no single approach is likely to be right for every child; rather, teachers may need to utilize a wide variety of teaching strategies for their students with ASD. Further, strategies may need to be modified to fit the developmental level and educational placement of the student. As each student is an individual, it is essential that teachers adapt teaching strategies to meet the student's individual interests, strengths, and needs. The intervention methods chosen should also allow the student to demonstrate progress toward his IFSP outcomes or IEP goals.

General Teaching Strategies

Programs that result in educational progress for students with ASD utilize motivational strategies and are typically introduced in a highly structured method in a one-to-one or small-group format with minimal distraction; attention to specific details of the skill; and a focus on consistency, repetition, and predictability.

For the student with ASD, verbal directions and unfamiliar materials often cause confusion that results in frustration and failure. As a result, many students with ASD become resistant to learning new skills. Therefore, it is necessary to identify and use teaching strategies that help motivate the student to learn. Many students with ASD have a limited repertoire of interests. Utilize these natural interests to capture the student's attention, to teach the student in a meaningful way, and as a reward for completed work. For example, if your student has an interest in computers, find an interesting way to use computers to teach new skills, or use the computer as a reward for task completion of a nonpreferred activity. Additional motivational strategies may include providing choices, changing the way in which instructions are given, modifying the appearance or presentation of a task, changing the length of a task, or adjusting the pacing of your instructional presentation.

When the students do not have skills in their repertoires or do not demonstrate skills often enough to provide evidence of mastery, a variety of teaching methods, such as discrete trials, pivotal response training, shaping, and prompting, may be employed to encourage the students to learn the new skills.

A discrete trial is a structured teaching strategy that is used to teach tasks or lessons that have been broken down into their simplest teachable components. It consists of four components: the instruction, the child's response, a consequence, and a brief pause.

Pivotal response training utilizes the discrete trial paradigm in lessons that are child directed. It also encourages teachers to create lesson plans and to work within the student's preferred activities.

Shaping, which is the reinforcement of successive approximations of the target behavior, is helpful when the students do not initially have the desired skills in their repertoires.

Prompting provides students with extra help to achieve the desired response. Prompting strategies may include verbal prompts, modeling, physical or gesture prompts, and the use of positional cues. Prompts can be used at the same time as instruction, during the student's response to help minimize errors, or after the student's incorrect response to demonstrate the correct answer. Although prompting strategies can be helpful in teaching new skills, it is essential to fade prompts over time to avoid prompt dependency.

Once new skills are acquired, it is important to fade out high levels of contextual support and systematically generalize the newly acquired behavior to more complex, natural environments and routines.

Communication Strategies

The communication abilities of students with ASD vary greatly, from students who are pre- or nonverbal to students with amazingly expressive vocabularies, and from students who have very limited receptive abilities to those who can understand complex conversations and instructions.

For preverbal and nonverbal students with ASD, a communication program may focus on teaching the student to communicate through gestures, speech, and/or an augmentative or alternative communication system. Alternative and augmentative communication systems such as sign language, visual symbol systems, communication boards, and voice output devices can provide an effective format for allowing students to communicate their wants and needs in any setting. Initiate augmentative and alternative communication options as soon as possible to ensure a method of reciprocal interaction and a system for teaching functional communication skills such as making requests, asking for help, protesting, and making choices. Early systems should be very functional and concrete. A typical progression for a visual-symbol communication system might be to move from a concrete to more abstract system. For example, you might start with objects or actual photographs, move next to colored photos and line drawings, and finally use printed words.

Whether teaching a student to communicate through gestures, speech, or an augmentative or alternative communication system, new skills should generally be introduced in quiet, nondistracting environments, with generalization occurring in more natural contexts where natural cues and reinforcements are available to make the skills meaningful and spontaneous. Utilize student interests to help motivate the child to initiate and use the communication system. For example, if a student has a favorite toy or book, the teacher may keep the material just out of reach but within sight of the student, thus encouraging the student to request the wanted item. Positively reinforce all communicative attempts and initiations.

In contrast to the pre- or nonverbal student, many students with ASD are able to utilize complex language. However, these students, along with their nonverbal peers, often demonstrate a significant impairment in pragmatic language. For example, students with ASD often struggle with such skills as having a social conversation; perceiving, understanding, and using gestures, facial expressions, and body language; initiating, maintaining, and closing conversations; as well as understanding and using social conventions and rituals. Pragmatic communication skills, an important component of the student's educational program, are taught effectively through direct instruction as well as through social skill instruction.

In addition to difficulty with pragmatic language, students with ASD also have difficulty understanding and comprehending complex language. When working with any student with ASD, a verbal or nonverbal student, it is important not to assume understanding. Teachers must closely monitor the student for receptive comprehension. Talk slowly and carefully. Some students will require simplified one- or two-step directions, while others will require extra time to process spoken language. Clearly state your instructions and directions, indicating what you expect the student to do rather than telling the student what not to do. Additionally, use proximity, gestures, and visual supports to enhance and clarify your spoken message.

While the content of language and communication instruction is similar for all children, the problems and strategies may differ. Work with your speech language pathologist to develop a comprehensive communication program.

Social Development Strategies

Most students with ASD want to have friends, fit in, and be an active member of the social world. However, they have difficulty reading, understanding, and responding to social cues. Indeed, social situations may baffle students with ASD. Because of their deficits in social understanding, students with ASD often develop, and then act upon, false beliefs or misperceptions about the social world, leading them to say or do things that inadvertently irritate and offend other people. Fortunately, a variety of approaches has been successfully demonstrated to teach students with ASD to understand and succeed in their social world.

Helping students with ASD to develop social understanding requires both systematic instruction as well as opportunities to practice the skills within naturally occurring routines. Rules, social stories, role-playing and scripts, cue cards and checklists, coaching, modeling, and friendship groups are all effective strategies for systematically teaching social skills.

Many classroom teachers find it helpful to teach and post the classroom social rules to help students understand the expectations of the classroom or other social situations. In writing rules, be sure to provide concrete, positively stated rules that are easy for the student to see and understand. Be sure to include a statement regarding why the rule is important. For example, "We use an inside voice so that students can finish their work." Including why a rule is important provides the social link that children with ASD often fail to make on their own. Review the rules on a regular basis and reward the child with positive contingencies for following the appropriate social rules. In addition to posting and reinforcing social rules, it is important to provide instruction around social situations that confuse the student.

Social stories, originally developed by Carol Gray, use visual instructional materials in the form of a short story to describe social situations that are confusing for the student. The goal of any social story is to share information at the student's developmental level regarding what is occurring in a given situation and why. Once written, the social story is read to or by the student to teach the new social skill and then again later to cue the student to practice the new skill. The team should develop a schedule to introduce, review, and fade the story.

In addition to social stories, scripting and role-playing are also effective strategies for teaching new social skills. Before introducing a student to a new social situation, it is often helpful to provide the child with a script of what to say and then role-play the situation. For example, a teacher may write a script teaching a student how to ask other children to play with him or her. The teacher and student might then role-play the scenario, practicing how to respond to a variety of different outcomes.

Once a student has begun to demonstrate success with social skills in a structured setting, it is essential to practice the skills within naturally occurring routines. Social skills and friendship groups provide a context for students to learn and to practice social skills in a supportive and structured environment. Additionally, many teachers find it helpful to assign a peer mentor or friend to help the student with ASD practice and use social skills in the natural environment. Whether through groups, peer mentors, or other systems, it is important to create opportunities for the student to practice newfound social skills successfully with peers and with other adults both in and out of the classroom.

Depending on training and background, a variety of professionals may have knowledge in teaching social development. Talk with your speech language pathologist, school counselor, or psychologist and special education teacher to develop a comprehensive social development program.

In addition to the previously mentioned teaching strategies, a number of individual treatment methodologies have been and continue to be developed for students with ASD. For a description of some of the most-cited treatment methodologies, refer to Chapter 5 of this book on interventions. Before choosing a teaching method or specific intervention strategy, Heflin and Simpson (1998) suggest that the IFSP or IEP team consider the following questions:

- Is the treatment published in peer-reviewed journals?
- Does the information regarding effectiveness come from a variety of sources?
- Are the studies that seem to validate the treatment's effectiveness of high quality?
- Is empirical validation available, or does the majority of the support come from personal testimonials?

- Do the proponents claim that the option will help almost everyone with ASD?
- How does this treatment rate in terms of restrictiveness and intensity?
- Are there less-restrictive/intensive alternatives that may be just as effective?
- Are there options that are better researched than this one?
- Does the treatment ignore the functional communication and socialization needs of this child?

5. Assessment of the Intervention

Prior to using any intervention, it is important to record a baseline of functioning in the particular area targeted for improvement. That is, it is important to assess or determine how the child is currently functioning in the area(s) of need. Once the goals and objectives are set, data are recorded to monitor progress in the program designed and can be used to improve the target area as well as to troubleshoot the program. The data are analyzed to determine if a lesson or educational intervention has been effective and what changes in the lesson or educational intervention need to be made. The IFSP or IEP team must determine how often data will be recorded and the criteria for determining when a particular intervention is unsuccessful and must be abandoned. Ongoing assessment of the child's skill via the data collection system determines the next set of goals and objectives.

6. Structuring the Environment

Although all students thrive on routine and predictability, students with ASD are especially sensitive to changes in the environment or routine. Structuring the environment for students with ASD increases calm, attention, and responsiveness to learning. Although the level of structure needed for each student will vary based on their age, diagnosis, and ability level, research has revealed that effective educational programs have structured environments that include the following:

- Physical structure
- Routines
- Visual supports

Physical Structure

Physical structure refers to the way each area in the classroom or school is set up and organized. To the student with ASD, who perceives the world differently or has unique sensory impairments, the school or classroom can be a confusing and overwhelming environment. Thus, the environment should be set up and organized with clear physical and visual boundaries. Boundaries such as carpets, bookcases, dividers, or study carrels are frames that visually identify an area, helping the student to understand where different activities take place and materials are stored. Consider providing a specific location for quiet activities and individual work activities. Once the various locations and boundaries are identified, signs, symbols, schedules, and choice boards can provide visual information on the rules and expectations of each area. Additionally, when planning the physical structure of the classroom, it is important to consider and minimize visual and auditory distractions, such as bright lights and noises (e.g., bells; children's loud voices; chairs scraping on the floor; and the humming of overhead projectors, lights, or computers).

Routines

Students with ASD are more socially responsive and attentive to learning and the environment when information is presented in a highly predictable and routine manner. Conversely, students with ASD can become easily overwhelmed by even minimal changes in their daily schedule or routine. To build independent work skills and to create a comfortable environment in which the student is ready to learn, develop routines and teach within them. For example, a routine for independent seatwork may be as simple as "First we work, and then we take a break." A routine for large-group instruction might be "First the teacher lectures, then the students do group practice problems, followed by independent seatwork, and then a break." Routines are also effective in teaching functional, leisure, and vocational skills. Of course, routines can become problematic if the student begins to demonstrate an obsession for sameness that results in negative behaviors when change occurs. To mitigate this stress, plan and prepare the student for potential changes in the routine by utilizing transition strategies, role-playing, and visual support systems.

Visual Supports

Students with ASD have strong visual skills. Visual organization of instruction and materials allows the student to utilize these visual learning strengths. Examples of helpful visual supports may include activity schedules and calendars, posted rules, choice boards, and other organizational methods as appropriate for individual students.

Activity schedules are a set of pictures or words that cue a student to participate in an activity. Depending on the student's age and ability level, an activity schedule may be a three-ring binder with only one activity on each page, it may be a partial- or full-day picture schedule, or it may be as complex as a Day-Timer planner/organizer or personal digital assistant (PDA). A mini-schedule is a set of pictures or words that cue children to the individual steps involved in a complex task. For example, students learning to wash their hands may have a mini-schedule breaking down the task of hand washing into four steps: turning on the water, washing hands, turning off the water, and drying hands. Other students may use a written mini-schedule for social studies class, breaking down the subject period into its component parts of silent reading, note taking during lecture, and small-group work.

Choice boards and menus are sets of pictures or words that visually communicate to the student with ASD what materials, rewards, or tasks are available to choose from. Choice boards can be effectively utilized to present a menu of leisure activities, work tasks, restaurant or food selection, work areas, places to visit, songs to sing, or any other activity that may be a part of the student's life or education. Using a choice board may alleviate frustration caused by being unable to communicate a request and motivate students by allowing them to have power over choosing which task or activity to participate in.

Other visual organizational methods may include organizing and labeling materials in the classroom or in the student's locker or book bag. Providing cue cards for rules and checklists for tasks, homework, or learning materials can be helpful as well.

7. Applying Functional Behavior Assessment to Problem Behavior

One goal of the educational program is to prevent the development of problem behaviors. As previously discussed, communication, social, academic, and motivational strategies, along with environmental modifications such as physical and visual organization, are effective strategies to utilize in teaching students with ASD and thus prevent many potential problem behaviors. If negative behaviors develop or continue, a functional behavior assessment is used to identify the purpose of the child's social-communicative behavior and the effect it has on others, based on interpretations of the child's intent and meaning. Once the functional behavior assessment is completed, an intervention is created. Effective interventions may include environmental modifications, curricular interventions, or instruction designed to match the student's identified needs. The intervention includes finding and teaching appropriate replacement behaviors to serve the same communicative function as the negative behavior exhibited. Positive behaviors are then reinforced to reduce the negative behaviors.

8. Transition

As discussed earlier, students with ASD often have difficulty with changes in the routine or the environment; this is especially true during unstructured periods, such as a planned or unplanned transitions. Consequently, students with ASD often need additional support and instruction in the skills that will allow them to be as independent as possible during transitions such as the following:

- Activity to activity
- Home to school
- School to home
- One grade/school to the next grade/school
- School to postschool environment

When planning for a transition, it is important to prepare the student for upcoming changes. When transitioning from activity to activity, provide verbal and visual warnings before ending an activity and use visual supports, such as schedules, to inform the student which activity will occur next. Transition objects, which provide a visual cue as to where the student is going, are often helpful for students transitioning from one activity to another. For example, a student may carry a spoon as a reminder that he or she is going to lunch.

When transitioning a student into a new grade, school, community, job or postschool environment, it is important to prepare the student for the upcoming change. Assess the new environment to determine what skills the student will need to be independent and successful and preteach those skills to the student. Talk with the student about the new environment and, if possible, allow the student to visit the new environment. If a site visit is not possible, consider videotaping, taking pictures, writing a social story, and compiling a list of expectations for the new environment. Additionally, meet with the staff members of the next setting to discuss the student's strengths and particular learning needs. Prepare the staff in the new setting by providing them with information on ASD and arranging to have them visit or learn about the student's current placement. If possible, arrange a meeting between the student and the new staff. When typical and major life transitions are systematically addressed and planned for, students with ASD are more likely to experience success, have confidence, and be more independent, creating a positive experience for everyone involved.

9. Opportunities With Peers

Students with ASD have significant difficulty in social and communicative interactions with others. Consequently, it is important for students with ASD to have regular and planned interactions with peers. Through peer contact, students with ASD may observe more appropriate models for social behavior, have access to responsive social partners, and engage in more normalized social experiences than would occur in the company of peers with ASD alone. However, it is important to recognize that merely placing a student with ASD in the same place as typically developing peers does not ensure acquisition of social and communication skills. According to Wagner (1999), the most effective methods for helping students with ASD gain essential social and communicative skills include the following:

- Play or recreational activities that have been appropriately structured
- Peers who have received training
- Teachers who actively prompt and reinforce interactions between the student with ASD and peers

10. Comprehensive Team Approach

As discussed throughout this manual, ASD is characterized by deficits in communication, behavior, and social skills. Consequently, an effective program for students with ASD requires the expertise and input of family members and staff from multiple disciplines trained to understand the implications of ASD. A comprehensive team approach includes parents and addresses personnel preparation issues, decision making, and follow-up provisions. It includes related services personnel, such as speech-language pathologists, psychologists, and/or occupational therapists, to address social and language skills. Furthermore, a comprehensive team includes special and general education teachers and/or paraeducators to ensure progress in meeting the individualized educational goals, objectives, and outcomes of each student. Working together, a comprehensive team ensures consistency of teaching and intervention techniques across individuals, lessons, and settings, increasing the likelihood of students with ASD to acquire, maintain, and generalize new skills and abilities.

7

Collaborating
With Parents

Developing and implementing effective educational programs that are meaningful for students with ASD require collaboration with parents. Parents of children with ASD work closely with professionals to obtain diagnoses, early intervention programs, and other resources and are usually knowledgeable about both the disorder and their children. Bringing the experiences and knowledge of parents to the program planning process not only enhances students' school success but also creates a climate for ongoing learning, communication, and collaboration.

A collaborative parent-school relationship is based on parents and teachers understanding each other's perspectives and realities. It is important for parents to have a clear understanding of their child's school program, the roles of staff members, and how individual classrooms meet the diverse needs of all the students.

It is equally important for teachers and school staff to have an understanding of the experiences families go through in living with children with ASD, the interventions they access, and the important role that schools play in families' lives. With these understandings and a commitment to collaboration, parents and teachers can work together to create positive and effective educational programs for students. Each family is unique and has different experiences obtaining a diagnosis and planning for and adapting to meet the needs of a child with ASD.

Obtain a Diagnosis

Obtaining a diagnosis is often the culmination of a long process that parents undergo while searching for an understanding of their child. Prior to seeking professional help, parents notice that their child's development is not progressing as expected and there is something different about the way their child behaves. Often the family physician is the first professional contacted. The following are common initial concerns that parents bring to their physicians regarding their child's development:

- The child may appear to have unusual listening patterns. He or she does not seem to respond to language yet seems to enjoy music. This concern may lead parents to explore whether the child has a hearing impairment.
- The child may seem aloof, make little eye contact, and resist attempts to bond with parents. This concern may lead parents to seek advice on how to form a closer attachment to their child.
- The child may have unusual eating and/or sleeping patterns. Many children with ASD are picky eaters, and parents are often concerned that they are not getting adequate nutrition. Other children with ASD have difficulty sleeping and are exhausted.
- The child may be slow developing language and communication skills.

Once concerns about a child's development are raised, there are many avenues physicians may take to investigate the issues. Specific diagnostic medical procedures, genetic testing, and referral to other professionals, such as speech-language therapists, occupational therapists, physiotherapists, and psychologists, are often initiated.

While early diagnosis is preferred, some children are diagnosed in later years. These are children whose early development and behavior was not conspicuously abnormal. It may be that once such a child entered the school system and was observed over time by a teacher familiar with normal child development, the autistic symptoms were detected. Other children may have had a history of social, language, learning, and/or behavioral difficulties and were assumed to have other kinds of disorders, such as attention deficit hyperactivity disorder (ADHD) or learning disabilities. However, careful observation over time revealed that the behavior was more accurately described as ASD.

Many parents are relieved to discover that there is an explanation for the behaviors their children exhibit. Many parents obtain a diagnosis as a way of determining what support and assistance they can access to best help their children. Although the diagnosis itself may be difficult to accept, the goal for most parents is to access appropriate intervention.

Adjust to the Diagnosis

Many books, articles, and research papers discuss the stages of acceptance families experience when they learn their children have ASD. Recent research studies indicate that people often experience multiple emotions and reactions that don't necessarily occur in discrete phases. Every family reacts differently to the discovery that a child has ASD and experiences its own unique way of coping and adjusting.

Adjustment often involves accepting the emotions experienced, gathering facts, and helping siblings and other family members understand the disorder. Acceptance occurs as parents learn more about ASD and realize they can take an active role in creating a positive future for their children. Gathering information, meeting other parents of children with ASD, identifying and using professional services, as well as advocating for their children are positive ways that parents can begin to adjust.

Developmental Stages and Family Stresses

All families go through different stages of development as children are born, grow up, and eventually move out on their own. Each stage brings new challenges and demands new accommodations.

Families of children with ASD often face these challenges more acutely, as they deal with the awareness that their children need different kinds of support and intervention at every stage. Parents often find themselves going through an acceptance cycle with each new phase of development. The transitions from preschool to elementary school, from elementary school to junior high and high school, and from high school to the adult world may be particularly challenging.

It is important that educators understand the perspectives and experiences that families bring to the home-school partnership. Many parents have a wealth of knowledge about the disorder, resources, and interventions and an overall understanding of what works for their individual child. Families may be experiencing stress and anxiety about the transition from one education system to another. It is also helpful for teachers to understand that other factors, such as family size, cultural background, socioeconomic status, and geographic location, affect the degree to which families are able to engage in the school-home partnership. Most parents are motivated to help their children but vary greatly in how they act on this motivation. Some parents have the time, temperament, educational background, or knowledge about ASD to work closely with the school staff. Other parents, although motivated and concerned about their children's development, may not be actively involved in their children's school programs. Educators need to be sensitive to the perspectives and beliefs families bring to the school context.

Create a Collaborative Home-School Partnership

Creating a collaborative home-school partnership must be carefully planned, keeping in mind the ultimate goal of working together to best meet the needs of students. Combining the strengths and knowledge of parents, who know their children best and have a history of supporting and advocating for their children, with the expertise of teachers creates a powerful partnership that directly benefits students. Collaboration between home and school can lead to improved academic and social success, positive attitudes and behavior toward school, better attendance, and improved parent-teacher communication.

A collaborative home-school partnership

- is an informed partnership where both parents and teachers understand the child's realities at home and at school;
- uses a team approach to program planning and development; and
- establishes a clear home-school communication plan.

Build an Informed Partnership

Being an informed partner in the home-school partnership requires that each participant have background information when beginning the collaboration process. Teachers need a general understanding of the nature of the student's disorder, the student's history, previous interventions and their effectiveness, and specific strengths and areas of growth. It is important for teachers to understand the experiences parents have gone through and have a global knowledge of the goals, dreams, and hopes that they hold for their children. Parents, in turn, need a thorough understanding of how the school system works, what program options are available, and how educational decisions are made at the school.

Establish a Team Approach

Collaborative partnerships involve a team approach. Programming for and meeting the unique needs of children with ASD involve complex decisions that parents and teachers cannot make in isolation. Team members can include administrators, special education consultants, teachers, teacher assistants, therapists, parents, and other community resource personnel. The school-based team is a critical part of the individualized program plan (IPP) process. Together, the team works to set meaningful academic and social goals and objectives, select strategies, develop positive behavior plans, and devise social programs to enhance peer relationships both at home and at school. The team can also plan and implement programs and inservice training to augment parent and teacher knowledge in the field of ASD.

Plan for Communication

The key to effective collaboration is communication. To maximize children's potential and generalize skills both at home and at school, parents and teachers need to communicate beyond the traditional parent-teacher interview modes. Parents and teachers need to work together to develop an effective communication plan. This plan should address how teachers and parents will communicate on a regular basis and how emergent concerns will be handled. A variety of communication methods should be considered, including daily diaries, home-school communication books, notes, letters, journals, newsletters, and regular phone calls.

Parents often want daily in-depth reporting about their children's learning and behavior. While meaningful communication between home and school is an essential ingredient for successful collaboration, it is important for teachers not to become overwhelmed with the task of reporting. It is often helpful for teachers and parents to prioritize specific areas to discuss on a daily basis. The communication protocol should be re-examined periodically to ensure that it continues to meet the needs of parents and teachers.

It is important for teachers to identify the amount and type of communication that parents require and to keep in mind that parents of students with ASD need to hear some positive news about their children. Like all parents, they appreciate personal messages that recognize their children's achievement and progress.

Facilitate Collaborative Relationships

Collaborating with parents often involves scheduling meetings for a variety of purposes. These meetings help teachers gain understanding of the child and family and the supports the family has in place. These meetings provide opportunities to clarify roles, set goals and objectives, and develop strategies and communication plans to plan and implement education programs effectively.

Parents may be working with other professionals who have valuable suggestions for education programming and developing behavior plans. Ask parents who they think should attend meetings to share information and provide ideas for strategies. Schools may also be able to access professionals within the school division who can contribute to the collaboration and planning process.

When Collaboration Becomes Difficult

At times, in spite of all good intentions, the parent-school partnership becomes difficult, and collaboration wanes. When this occurs, it is helpful for educators and parents to work toward understanding each other's perspectives to determine the barriers to collaboration and ensure that the child will not be negatively impacted.

General principles of mediation can be used to maintain and improve the home-school relationship. Identifying educators' and parents' mutual concerns and goals is a starting point for working together. Too often, parents and teachers become fixed in their positions and lose sight of their goals. When the focus is on the needs of the child, parents and teachers may be able to move beyond fixed positions to work creatively and cooperatively toward solutions.

Parents and school personnel may have differing views of children and their needs. Take constructive steps to reach a shared understanding by identifying the underlying needs of parents. Listen to and incorporate parents' perspectives concerning long- and short-term goals for their children to help narrow the gap between opposing views. Be cognizant that the language used to describe children takes into account the whole child—abilities, strengths, and aspirations, as well as needs.

In some instances, it may be helpful to enlist an objective, mutually acceptable third party to facilitate collaboration. Collaboration will be enhanced when parents and school staff are committed to working together for the best interests of children. Parents and teachers are the two most powerful influences in children's lives. Working together in a collaborative partnership promotes meaningful and effective learning.

8

Effective Programming for Young Children With ASDs

Ages 3–5

The positive outcome of early intervention programming for any child with developmental delays/disabilities has been documented in numerous research articles and publications. However, unlike children with many other developmental disabilities, children with ASD are typically not diagnosed until between the ages of 2 and 3, as there are no medical tests to make a definitive diagnosis of ASD at an earlier age. Many medical professionals prefer to take a wait-and-see approach due to the wide range of "normalcy" in young children. Thus, early intervention programming can often be delayed for these children, resulting in the loss of several critical years of intensive intervention during which significant

Material from this chapter appears courtesy of Susan Stokes under a contract with CESA 7 and funded by a discretionary grant from the Wisconsin Department of Public Instruction. *Effective programming for young children with autism (Ages 3–5).* Retrieved on August 30, 2007 from http://www.specialed.us/autism/early/ ear11.htm. Used with permission.

developments in the brain are occurring. Due to this time factor, once a diagnosis is given, early intervention programming becomes crucial to address the child's needs in all developmental areas and, most importantly, to develop the child's ability to function independently in all aspects of life.

Fundamental Features

The fundamental features necessary for a successful early childhood program for children with ASD are as follows:

- Curriculum content
- Highly supportive teaching environments and generalization strategies
- Need for predictability and routine
- Functional approach to problem behavior
- Transition planning from early childhood program to elementary school
- Family involvement

Each of these components will be discussed in detail in this chapter.

Curriculum Content

The curricular areas to be focused on in an early childhood program should address the core features and characteristics of ASD. The goals and objectives to address each curricular area should be highly individualized for each child's developmental level and learning strengths and weaknesses. Knowledge of typical child development is also crucial in providing a guideline for intervention in the curricular areas. The following curricular areas have been identified as essential to meeting the needs of young children with ASD.

Attending Skills

A common feature of ASD is the children's significant difficulties in interpreting and prioritizing the importance of various external and internal stimuli continually bombarding them (e.g., a fly buzzing around the room; internal perseverative thoughts, such as recitation of math facts). As a result, many of these children can exhibit the following behaviors:

- *Variable attending skills:* The children demonstrate attending skills that vary significantly, depending upon their interests. For example, they attend well to what is interesting or "makes sense," such as the computer, videos, puzzles, etc., but attend poorly to large-group listening activities.
- *Difficulty in shifting attention from one stimulus to another:* For example, if the child is engaged in a visual perceptual task of putting a puzzle together, he or she may not be able to shift attention to focus on an auditory directive given by the teacher.
- *Difficulty attending in situations where there are multiple stimuli.* Because the child with ASD has significant difficulty shifting attention, as well as prioritizing stimuli, attending to the "essential information" is challenging. For example, if the child's focused attention is on "sitting appropriately in a small-group setting," he or she may not be able to focus on the information being taught by the teacher.

Imitation

Imitation is a critical developmental skill for children with ASD, as learning throughout life is based on the foundation of being able to imitate. The ability to imitate impacts learning in all areas, including social skills and communication. Various imitation skills must be specifically and directly taught to the child with ASD. These include the following:

- Imitating fine and gross motor movements
- Imitating actions on objects
- Imitating designs with manipulatives
- Imitating sounds and words

Communication (Understanding and Use)

Children with ASD exhibit significant communication difficulties with both comprehending and expressing language appropriately. Many children at the early intervention level have not learned the "power" of communication—that is, the cause and effect of communication. They have not developed the "intent" to communicate. For example, some children will try to obtain a desired item themselves and not seek out others for assistance. Children with ASD have difficulty understanding that communication is an intentional exchange of information between two or more people. Therefore, to be taught this intent to communicate at this early intervention level, many children with ASD must be "tempted" to communicate with their highly desired objects and actions.

Play Skills With Toys

Children with ASD exhibit marked difficulty engaging in appropriate play skills with toys. Play skills with toys can range among the following levels:

- *No interaction:* The child shows no interest in touching or holding toys.
- *Manipulative/explorative play:* The child holds and gazes at toys; mouths, waves, shakes, or bangs toys; stacks blocks or bangs them together; lines up objects.
- *Functional play:* The child puts teacup to mouth, puts brush to hair, connects train sections and pushes train, arranges pieces of furniture in dollhouse, constructs a building with blocks.
- *Symbolic/pretend play:* The child pretends to do something or to be someone else with an intent that is representational, including role-playing (e.g., child makes hand move to mouth, signifying drinking from teacup; makes a puppet talk; uses a toy person or doll to represent self; uses block as a car accompanied by engine sounds).

Social Play/Social Relations

A core feature of ASD is difficulty understanding and engaging in social interactions. At the early intervention level, children with ASD typically exhibit significant difficulty engaging in social play with peers. Social play skills with peers can range among the following levels:

- *Isolation:* The children appear to be unaware of or oblivious to others. They may occupy themselves by watching anything of momentary interest.
- *Orientation:* The children have an awareness of the other children, as evidenced by looking at them or at their play materials or activities. However, the children do not enter into play.
- *Parallel/proximity play:* The children play independently beside, rather than engaging with, the other children. There is simultaneous use of the same play space or materials as peers.

- *Common focus:* The children engage in activities directly involving one or more peers, including informal turn taking, giving and receiving assistance and directives, and active sharing of materials. There is a common focus or attention on the play.

Typically developing peer models are essential to facilitate developmentally appropriate social behavior for children with ASD.

Highly Supportive Teaching Environments and Generalization Strategies

The previously noted curricular areas must be taught in an environment that takes into consideration the unique features and characteristics associated with ASD. The specific skills per curricular area should be taught in a highly supportive and structured teaching environment, then systematically generalized to more functional, natural environments. Features of the environments that should be addressed include the following.

Physical Environment

Due to difficulties in appropriately processing and modulating incoming sensory stimulation, the physically structured environment should provide environmental organization for children with ASD.

> **Furniture arrangement:** Environmental organization includes clear physical and visual boundaries, which (a) help the child to understand where each area begins and ends and (b) minimize visual and auditory distractions. Each area of the classroom (or other environment) should be clearly visually defined through the arrangement of furniture (e.g., bookcases, room dividers, office panels, shelving units, file cabinets, tables, rugs, etc.).

Children with ASD generally do not automatically segment their environments like typically developing children. Large, wide-open areas can be extremely challenging for children with ASD. They do not understand what is to occur in each area, where each area begins and ends, and how to get to a specific area by the most direct route. Strategically placing furniture to clearly visually define specific areas will decrease the child's tendency to wander/run randomly from area to area.

Visual Distractions

Visual distractions can be minimized by painting the entire environment (walls, ceilings, bulletin boards, etc.) a muted color (e.g., off-white) as well as markedly limiting the amount of visual "clutter" present in most classrooms in the form of art projects, seasonal decorations, and classroom materials. Reduction of visual clutter can be accompanied by using sheets/curtains to cover classroom materials (including equipment, such as a computer or TV/VCR) or by removing unnecessary equipment/materials from the classroom or to an area not in the student's view. Certain fluorescent lighting can be visually distracting to some children with ASD, but natural lighting via windows can provide an easy solution. Through the use of blinds, curtains, or shades, the amount of light coming into the environment can easily be controlled, thus creating a warm and calm environment.

Auditory Distractions

Reducing auditory distractions in a physically structured environment can be achieved through the use of carpeting, lowered ceilings, and acoustical tiles; turning off the public address system or covering it with foam to mute the sound; and providing headphones for appropriate equipment, such as the computer or tape players.

A physically structured environment will create an easily understood, predictable, and thus calming environment for the child with ASD. As a result the child's attention to the most relevant information for learning will be maximized.

Visual Support Strategies

Visual support strategies refer to the presentation of information in a visually structured manner. These strategies are effective in helping children with ASD understand what is expected of them and how to function appropriately. These strategies support the children's strongest processing area—visual. The visual cues help the child to focus on the relevant and key information. Visual support strategies help children with ASD learn more effectively. These strategies also minimize stress and anxiety by helping children grasp their environment. Visual support strategies in an early intervention program can include the following:

- Schedules
- Directions (e.g., self-help skills—tooth brushing, hygiene, washing hands)
- Forewarning/foreshadowing
- Independent work activities
- Teaching rules/alternative behaviors
- Increasing language comprehension skills
- Expressive communication skills
- Making choices
- Turn taking
- Waiting
- Attending
- Academic/readiness areas

Need for Predictability and Routine

Another diagnostic feature of ASD is the child's strict adherence to routines and the need for sameness in the environment. Early childhood programs that are highly structured, consistent, and routine can best meet the child's needs by taking into account this feature of ASD. Just as with visual support strategies, programs that are predictable and routine centered also minimize children's stress and anxiety by helping them to understand the environment better.

Functional Approach to Challenging Behaviors

The most effective approach to addressing challenging behaviors in children with ASD is proactive. One can prevent the development of challenging behaviors by creating appropriate and meaningful learning environments that do not generate the stress, anxiety, and frustration typically experienced by children with ASD. Due to the characteristics of ASD, areas such as language comprehension, expressive language, sensory processing, resistance to change, preference for familiar routines and consistency, organization, attending to salient stimuli, and distractibility often cause stress.

Using the fundamental features of an early childhood program will assist in proactively addressing challenging behaviors. If and when challenging behaviors persist, they should be addressed through a functional assessment of the behaviors. Again, the unique features and characteristics associated with ASD should be considered in the functional behavioral assessment to determine how they might be contributing to the challenging behavior.

Transition Planning: From an Early Childhood Program to Elementary School

Due to difficulties in making transitions, accepting change, and generalizing previously acquired skills, the child with ASD may experience significant challenges in transitioning from an early childhood program to a primary elementary program. Therefore, several critical components have been identified to assist the child in making this transition successfully.

- *Develop independent functioning skills:* The initial development of independent functioning skills is an important factor in preparing the child for elementary school. It is critical to begin teaching children with ASD independent functioning skills as soon as they enter an early childhood program. These skills will assist them throughout their lives. Independent functioning in all curricular areas should be addressed (e.g., communication, social relations, play, self-help/daily living skills, attending, navigating the school environment, etc.).
- *Determine an appropriate placement:* The child's early childhood program should take an active role in assisting the parents and school districts in finding an appropriate placement for each child transitioning from an early childhood program to an elementary school. Factors to be considered include class size, degree of classroom structure, teaching style, and physical environment.
- *Staff training:* It is critical for the elementary school staff, who will be directly working with the child, to be trained in the unique features and characteristics common to ASD. The training should also include strategies directly applicable to a child with ASD.

Visitations to the child's early childhood program by the elementary school staff are also important so that the early childhood staff can assist in providing direct, individual, child-specific information and training if necessary. In addition, the early childhood staff should visit the elementary school to determine skill areas that may need to be addressed prior to the child's transition. Early childhood staff can also help assess the physical environment and determine if any adaptations/modifications should be considered.

It is also suggested that the entire school professional staff partic-ipate in a general inservice or receive information regarding the unique features and characteristics of ASD, so all staff members can more readily understand the child who will be entering their school.

Visitation to Elementary School Placement

It is suggested that children's transitions to their elementary schools placements be accomplished gradually. This can occur in a number of ways. As mentioned previously, the children can become adjusted to the new teaching staff in their familiar and comforting early childhood environments when the elementary school staffs visit the children's early childhood programs. After this is accomplished, the children can begin to visit the elementary schools on a gradual basis, accompanied by familiar adults from their early childhood programs. The amount of time that the children spend in the elemen-tary school placement is gradually increased. This procedure tends to work best in that, if any difficulties arise when the children are in the elementary school placement, these difficulties can still be addressed in the familiar and comforting early childhood environment.

Family Involvement

Parallel Training of Parent/Family and Staff

The parent/family should be informed by school staff of strate-gies that are being used successfully at school. In turn, the parents should inform school staff of successful home strategies. This mutual sharing of information/ideas can be accomplished through the following:

- Monthly home visits
- Monthly staff/family support meetings
- Daily home-school communication notebook
- Phone calls
- School visitations

Parents as Visitors or Volunteers

Many parents may wish to visit or volunteer time at their child's early childhood program. This can be accomplished in many different ways, depending upon the parents' time schedules, the needs of the teacher, as well as the individual needs of the children. Some children can become quite anxious and upset when their own parents are in the classroom environment. The children perceive this as a "change"; that is, their parents are associated with the home environment and not the classroom. In such cases, parents can volunteer by making materials, copies, etc. outside the classroom. Also, many schools have policies and procedures regarding visitations and volunteering, which should be consulted.

Other Program Features

Other program features that may greatly contribute to the success of a child's early childhood program are the following:

- *Team-teaching approach:* A successful approach to meeting the unique and individualized needs of children with ASD is utilization of a team-teaching concept. In this approach, staff members combine their specialized skill areas to team-teach the students in the program. Various professionals and paraprofessionals can be part of this teaching team (e.g., speech/language pathologist, occupational therapist, early childhood teacher, certified occupational therapy assistant, and classroom aides). Although all members will contribute greatly to the team regarding their specialty areas, in an ideal team-teaching environment, it should be difficult for visitors to distinguish the various specialty areas of the teachers in the classroom. Utilization of team-teaching provides the child with ongoing, consistent, and individualized focus in all skill areas.
- *Individualized program:* The individualized education plan (IEP) is the blueprint for successfully meeting the needs of the child with ASD. Each child's daily program is based on his or her specific needs (IEP goals and objectives) and will be different from that of every other child in the classroom.
- *Data-driven:* Ongoing data collection should take place to support progress toward each child's IEP goals and objectives, to assist in determining daily programming, and to substantiate the overall efficacy of the child's IEP.
- *Typically developing peers:* It is critical for an early childhood program to have ready access to typically developing peers to provide models and support for the child with ASD. Individualized mainstreaming can take place in various ways For example, for a particular child with ASD, 1–2 peers can

come into the early childhood classroom to act as peer models when focusing on structured play skills, such as turn taking or imitating actions on objects. Also, the child may be participating in day care or another preschool setting, or even kindergarten, where typically developing peers are present. A variety of options are available to accomplish this objective.

In conclusion, well-planned and implemented early childhood programs are cost-effective in the long term; children with ASD who have benefited from such programs require less-intensive services later on. Most importantly, appropriate early childhood programs help children with ASD acquire the independent functioning skills that will benefit every aspect of their lives.

9

Teaching Students
With ASD

Instructional Approaches

No single instructional method for teaching students with ASD is successful for all students. Also, students' needs change over time, making it necessary for teachers to try other approaches. This chapter contains information about important areas of instruction and instructional approaches that have proved successful for teachers working with students with ASD.

Visual Approaches

The most strongly recommended approach for teaching students with ASD is to use visual aids. Students often demonstrate relative strengths in concrete thinking, rote memory, and understanding of visual-spatial relationships while they demonstrate difficulties in abstract thinking, social cognition, communication, and attention. Pictographic and written cues can often help the student to learn, communicate, and develop self-control.

One of the advantages of using visual aids is that students can use them for as long as they need to process the information. In contrast, oral information is transient: once said, the message is no longer available. Oral information may pose problems for students who have difficulty processing language and who require extra time. In addition, it may be difficult for the student with ASD to attend to relevant information and to block out background stimulation. Using visual supports enables the individual to focus on the message.

Visual aids and symbols range in complexity from simple and concrete to abstract. The continuum moves from real object or situation, to facsimile, color photograph, color picture, black-and-white picture, line drawing, and finally to graphic symbol and written language.

Objects are the most simple, concrete form of aid. Graphic symbols, although far along the continuum in terms of complexity and abstraction, have been widely successful with students with ASD. Software packages that provide quick access to graphic symbols and the ability to create customized symbols are available.

Visual supports can be used in a variety of ways in the classroom. However, to be successful, they must fit the student's level of comprehension by being at the appropriate point on the continuum of complexity. Using a line drawing to support learning when the student needs color photographs to comprehend will only frustrate everyone.

Taking this caution into account, visual supports are very useful and can be employed to accomplish the following:

- *Organize the student's activity.* Supports may be daily schedules, mini-schedules, activity checklists, calendars, or choice boards.
- *Provide directions or instructions for the student.* Visual displays of classroom assignments, file cards with directions for specific tasks and activities, pictographs, and written instructions for learning new information assist the student in understanding the organization of the environment, as does labeling of objects, containers, signs, lists, charts, and messages.
- *Support appropriate behavior.* Posted rules and representations signal steps of routines and teach social skills, and pictorial representations of social stories, developed for a specific situation for the individual student, depict social situations with the social cues and appropriate responses.
- *Teach self-control.* For example, pictographs can provide cues for behavior expectations.

The key question to ask when planning an activity or giving an instruction is this: How can this information be presented in a simple visual format? Choose visual aids on the basis of an understanding of the student and his abilities and responses.

Provide Precise, Positive Praise While the Student Is Learning

Give students precise information about what they do right or well; for example, "great coloring" or "good finishing of that math problem." Generalized praise may result in unintended learning that is hard to reverse. Students with ASD may learn on one trial, so directing the praise to the very specific behavior is important: "Sal, you are doing very well at multiplying these numbers." Superstitious learning can occur if students mistakenly connect something they are doing with the praise. Saying "Sal, you are doing very well," when Sal is also swinging his feet while he does the math assignment might connect the feet swinging with the general praise.

Use Meaningful Reinforcements

Reinforcers can be anything from praise to tangible objects that increase the behavior the student is to learn. Students with ASD may not be motivated by common reinforcers that work with other students. They might prefer some time spent alone, time to talk to a preferred staff member, a trip to the cafeteria, an exercise routine (such as going for a walk), time to play with a desired object, music, playing in water, getting to perform a favorite routine, items that provide specific sensory stimulation, or sitting at the window.

It is important to know what works as reinforcement for each child. A preference profile that identifies the activities or other reinforcers that are preferred by the student can be helpful. This "likes and dislikes" list can be developed with the help of the family and shared with all service providers.

Plan Tasks at an Appropriate Level of Difficulty

Students with ASD may be particularly vulnerable to anxiety and intolerant of feelings of frustration if they cannot perform the tasks assigned. Increasing the level of difficulty gradually and scaffolding or supporting learning (particularly with visual information rather than solely oral explanations) will assist in minimizing the student's frustration.

Use Age-Appropriate Materials

It is important to honor the dignity of students with ASD through the choice of instructional materials. Even if the instruction must be modified significantly, the learning materials should be appropriate to the age of the student.

Provide Opportunities for Choice

Because students with ASD may be frequently frustrated by their inability to make themselves understood, they need instruction and practice in making good choices for themselves. Many parts of their lives may necessarily be highly structured and controlled by adults.

Sometimes students continue to choose one activity or object because they do not know how to choose another. Acceptable methods of providing choice for students who have limited ability to communicate need to be developed on an individual basis. Direct teaching of making choices may be helpful. Choice should be limited to one or two preferred activities until the students grasp the concept of choice. Open-ended choices will not enhance students' skills at making choices and may only frustrate them.

Break Down Oral Instructions Into Small Steps

When providing instruction for students with ASD, teachers should avoid long strings of verbal information. As discussed above, supporting oral instruction with visual cues and representations will help students to understand.

Pay Attention to Processing and Pacing Issues

Students with ASD may need longer to respond than other students. This may be linked to cognitive and/or motor difficulties. Students with ASD may need to process each discrete piece of the message or request and, therefore, need extra time to respond. Providing extra time generally and allowing for ample time between giving instructions and student responses are both important tactics for supporting students with ASD.

Use Concrete Examples and Hands-On Activities

Teach abstract ideas and conceptual thinking using specific examples. Also, vary the examples so that the concept is not accidentally learned as applying in only one way.

Use Task Analysis

Teachers and parents may need to break complex tasks down into subtasks and reinforce in small, teachable steps. For each step of a complex task, the student needs to have the requisite skills. These subskills may need to be taught and reinforced in sequence. For example, when teaching a self-help skill, such as brushing teeth, the task may need to be broken down into subskills: getting the toothbrush and toothpaste, turning on the water, wetting the toothbrush, unscrewing the lid of the toothpaste, putting the toothpaste on the toothbrush, etc. Life skills, social skills, and academic skills can all be analyzed and approached as tasks and subtasks, with each step taught and then linked to the next in a chain of subtasks.

Use Discrete Trial Methods

Using prompts to help students learn is an important element of instruction for some students with ASD. Prompts may be physical, gestural, or verbal. They should only be used as long as they are needed, as students can become dependent on prompts. When using the discrete trial strategy, the instructor presents the stimulus for the desired behavior (gives the directions or instructions) and prompts the student. The student responds, and then the instructor provides consequences based on behavioral principles. The prompt is often designed to model the desired behavior or assist the student in performing it.

Introduce Unfamiliar Tasks in a Familiar Environment When Possible

When it is not possible to introduce unfamiliar tasks in a familiar environment, prepare the individual for the new task and environment using aids such as pictures, videotapes, and/or social stories.

Organize Teaching Materials and the Situation to Highlight What Is Important

Use organization aids and visual supports to:

- help the student attend to pertinent information, and
- teach new tasks.

For example, remove extraneous materials from the desk or table before attempting to teach a skill. Or present only the text you want read rather than the whole book. Highlight the key words, such as character names in the text, so they are noticed.

Encourage Independent Effort and Incorporate Proactive Measures to Reduce the Likelihood of Becoming Dependent on Prompts

When students with ASD are constantly supported, they may never develop the capacity to act independently. Since independence is a desired goal for all students, instruction should include strategies to decrease the need for adult prompting. Strategies include the following:

- Using visual aids to decrease reliance on physical and verbal prompts from the parent, teacher, or teacher assistant
- Planning ways to fade prompts
- Ensuring that the adult is not always positioned close to the student and that the same adults are not always present. Positioning the adult away from the student and changing teacher assistants may help to avoid dependency.
- Providing visual organizational aids, such as schedules, task outlines, checklists, and charts, and involving the student in developing and using them, if feasible

- Providing instruction to increase the student's awareness of environmental cues
- Teaching in the environments containing the cues and reinforcement that prompt and maintain the behavior

Direct and Broaden Fixations Into Useful Activities

If the student is fixated on an object or a topic, such as a color or shape, use it to teach a concept. A whole week's learning activities in writing and math can be centered on one topic—this is using creative theme-based learning activities taken to the extreme.

Know the Individual and Maintain a List of Strengths and Interests

Family members can provide valuable information for teachers about what students know and do at home or in the community. These interests and skills can be built upon both for instruction and for reinforcing successful learning and behavior.

Develop Talent and Interest Areas

If the student demonstrates a particular interest and strength in a specific area (e.g., music, drama, art, graphics, computer), provide opportunities to develop further expertise in that area. This approach may not only provide enjoyment and success but may also lead to the development of skills for future employment.

10

Teaching Students With ASD

Strategies for Classroom Management

No single classroom management approach is successful for all students. Students' needs change over time, making it necessary for teachers to try various approaches. This chapter contains information about important areas of classroom management strategies that have proved successful for teachers working with students with ASD.

Provide a Structured, Predictable Classroom Environment

Structuring the classroom environment is not to be confused with an authoritarian approach. The environment should be structured to provide consistency and clarity so that students know where things belong and what is expected of them in a specific situation and can anticipate what comes next.

Provide a Customized Visual Daily Schedule

The individualized schedule for a student with ASD should fit comfortably into the overall classroom schedule. Vary tasks to prevent boredom and alternate activities to reduce anxiety and possibly prevent some inappropriate behaviors. For example, alternate familiar, successful experiences with less-preferred activities. It may be helpful to alternate large-group activities with opportunities for calming down in a quiet environment. In addition, incorporating physical activity and exercise at points throughout the day is helpful.

All planned activities can be charted in a visual form and posted at or near the desks of students with ASD so that they can understand changes in activities and know what to expect. The students can be helped to learn to use the schedule independently, and staff can direct students to the schedule when it is time to change activities to smooth transition times.

An inventory of the possible sensory factors can be used to help minimize the negative effect that sensory information may be having on students with ASD. Parents and others who have experience with the student will be a valuable source of information about sensory difficulties. Here are some questions to ask and other points to consider when developing an inventory.

Auditory

- Are there fans, loudspeakers, fire alarms, several people talking at once, air conditioners, bells, dogs barking, or scraping?
- What is the general sound level and the predictability and repetitiveness of sounds?
- What can be done to minimize the negative effect these stimuli may have on the student with ASD?
- Consider the individual's comprehension of verbal information and the time typically required to process auditory information and to shift attention between auditory stimuli.

Visual

- Are there distractions, such as light, movement, reflection, or background patterns, that affect the student's ability to attend to the learning activity?

- Consider the eye level of the student, the position of the teacher in relation to the student, and distractions that may interfere with attention.
- Also, consider the time required to shift visual attention. Careful attention to aversive visual stimuli and attempts to reduce the effect of these stimuli will assist managing the student's behavior and help the student learn.

Tactile

- Are there textures that seem to be aversive?
- Are temperatures appropriate to minimize negative effect on the student?
- Does the student demonstrate a need to explore through touch yet avoid being touched?
- What is the level of ability or defensiveness in the use of certain objects intended to support instruction?

Vestibular

- Consider the student's need to move and exercise.
- What are the individual's reactions to movement?
- How can the student's program incorporate needed movement without unduly jeopardizing the attention and learning of other students in the class?

Gustatory and Olfactory

- Consider the preferences in taste and smell of foods and other materials.
- Decisions about activities should include consideration of the student's responses to the smell of materials.
- Teaching the appropriate behavior for snack or mealtimes will be affected by these preferences.

Note Aspects of the Tasks and Activities That Create Frustration

Examine the instructional plan and noninstructional activities for problem areas that may result in sensory overload or frustration for the student. Make available sensory experiences that are calming for the student to accompany potentially frustrating tasks. Whenever possible, adapt tasks and materials to promote successful participation. When feasible, decrease environmental distractions and reduce activities that confuse, disorient, or upset the student and interfere with learning.

Provide Relaxation Opportunities and Areas

It may be necessary to have a calm, quiet, designated area where the student can go to relax. Relaxing for some students with ASD may mean engaging in repetitive behaviors that have a calming effect. In some cases, students who crave certain repetitive movement, such as rocking or other self-stimulating movements, can be provided with a time and space where this movement is permitted.

Provide Opportunities for Meaningful Contact With Peers Who Have Appropriate Social Behavior

It will be necessary to teach appropriate social behavior and to provide the student with situation-specific expectations for behavior.

Opportunities for contact with peers may include the following:

- Involving the student in shared learning arrangements. Examples include pairing the student with buddies for walking down the hall, on the playground, and during other unstructured times. Also, it is important to vary peer buddies across time and activities to prevent dependence on one child.
- Involving peers in providing individualized instruction
- Arranging cross-age peer supports/buddies by assigning an older student to assist the student with ASD
- Pairing students while attending special school events, such as assemblies and clubs
- Facilitating involvement in afterschool or extracurricular activities

If your school has an arrangement in which a class of older students is paired with a younger class, ensure that the older student with ASD is also paired and provide the necessary supports for success.

Plan for Transitions and Prepare the Student for Change

Students with ASD often find changes in activity, setting, or planned routine very stressful. Visual schedules can be used to help them understand and cooperate with necessary changes. Social stories with illustrations can also be used to prepare the student for new situations.

11

Teaching Students With ASD

Strategies for Communication Development

Expanding the communication skills of students with ASD is one of the greatest challenges for teachers and families. Most people are unaware of the complexity of normal communication, because children develop these skills automatically, usually by the age of 3 or 4.

Many students with ASD have not developed the skills they need for spontaneous communication and must therefore be taught. Helping students with ASD develop communication skills—so that they can express their wants and needs, interact socially, share information, express emotions, and protest or escape aversive situations—is a priority. Programs to facilitate the development of communication may begin in structured settings; however, promoting generalization and facility in using language requires that interventions take place in natural settings.

Functional language skills are best taught in the social context where they will be used and where they have real meaning. The classroom and school environments provide a wealth of opportunities for developing functional communication within social contexts and promoting generalization. However, opportunity alone will not address the communication needs of the student with ASD. The specific skills requiring instruction and strategies for developing the targeted skills must be identified.

The school team, parents, and specialized professionals should collaborate to identify communication goals and objectives for the student with ASD. The planned interventions should be based on the abilities and needs of the student. The speech and language pathologist can assist in assessment of communication skills and provide suggestions and strategies tailored to the unique needs and characteristics of the student.

Here are some general suggestions for assisting with communication:

- Focus on developing interaction and communication in the environments in which the child participates (e.g., classroom, playground, gym).
- Use sentences to talk to the student. Keep in mind that you are modeling speech as well as trying to communicate with the student.
- Use vocabulary appropriate to the student's comprehension capability. For students with more severe communication disability, choose familiar, specific, and concrete words and repeat as necessary.
- Use language that is clear, simple, and concise. Figures of speech and irony or sarcasm will only confuse students with communication difficulties.
- Allow time for the student to process the information. It may be necessary to talk more slowly or to pause between words. The pace of speech depends on the ability of the individual student.

Learning to Listen

Students with ASD often need structured lessons on how to listen. Reinforcing listening efforts rather than assuming that listening is an expected and automatic behavior may be necessary. Breaking listening down into components for the student and reinforcing each component may be helpful—for example, teaching the student to face the speaker, look at one spot (which does not mean they must make eye contact), and place hands in a planned position and praising or otherwise rewarding each step.

Developing Oral Language Comprehension

Use visual input to aid comprehension of oral speech. Visual aids may help obtain and maintain the student's attention. Accompanying spoken language with relevant objects, pictures, and other visual supports can help with comprehension. Experienced teachers of students with ASD suggest the use of photographs to support understanding of the content of oral communication. Interestingly, many students with ASD use reading to support oral comprehension rather than the expected reverse of using oral language to support reading. This makes reading instruction even more significant for these students.

When working with students who are higher functioning, it is easy to assume that they understand information, particularly if they are able to repeat it. However, even though there may be good recall, the student may not grasp the intended meaning. It is important to check for comprehension.

Developing Oral Language Expression

Students with ASD may not develop traditional oral language, but most do develop some form of communication. It is important that people involved with the student have a thorough knowledge of the student's form of expression and that they adjust their expectations for communication accordingly. For students with limited oral expression, teachers and families should accept limited verbal attempts and nonverbal behavior as communicative. A customized communication dictionary is a very useful tool in which staff and parents can document what the student says and what is meant, along with planned adult responses to language attempts.

Even those students with ASD who do have oral language may not add to their working oral vocabularies easily. Teachers and parents will need to teach new vocabulary in a variety of contexts using a visually based approach. Students need to be taught that:

- everything in our world has a name;
- there are different ways of saying the same thing;
- words can be meaningful in a variety of contexts; and
- learning to use words will help them communicate their needs and desires.

Students who rely on pictorial representations to communicate will need to learn that a drawing or representation has a name and that it can give direction, or tell us what to do. Understanding this is essential for visual systems to provide meaningful communication. The student's education program should include situations that encourage different types of expression, such as the following:

- Requests (e.g., for food, toys, or help)
- Negation (e.g., refusing food or a toy, protesting when asked to do something, or indicating when the student wants to stop)
- Commenting (e.g., labeling pictures in books or objects from a box, greeting people, or engaging in play activities)

Developing Conversation Skills

Virtually all people with ASD have difficulty with the pragmatics of communication—the interpretation and use of language in social situations. Even those individuals who have a good vocabulary and appear to have a command of the language may have a restricted understanding of social and conversational interactions.

For some students, it may be necessary to provide structured teaching to develop the oral language needed for social and communicative play. This can be done by providing structured play opportunities that incorporate the student's interests. Modeling, physical prompts, visual cues, and reinforcement can be used to facilitate attention, imitation, communication, and interaction. To facilitate social communication, structure interactions around the student's activity preferences and routine. Also, encourage informal and formal communicative social exchanges during the day.

Simple drawings are an effective strategy for teaching conversation skills. These drawings illustrate what people say and do and emphasize what they may be thinking. A set of symbolic drawings can be used to represent basic conversational concepts, such as listening, interrupting, using loud and quiet words, talking, and thoughts. Colors may be incorporated to represent the emotional context. Pictures with scripts can also be used to develop conversation skills and communication appropriate to specific social contexts and situations.

People with ASD have difficulty understanding subtle social messages and rules and have problems interpreting the nonverbal communication of others. It may be helpful to provide the student with a concrete rule when one exists and to present it in a visual format by writing it down or incorporating it into a social story or comic strip conversation. Students also need opportunities for social interactions and community-based experiences to practice these skills.

Echolalia

Some children with ASD demonstrate *echolalia,* the literal repetition of words or phrases from language of other people. Young children use echolalia as part of normal language development. However, in ASD, some learners seem to stop developing at this level of language growth.

Echolalia can be immediate or delayed; that is, the student can repeat what was just heard or can repeat it later, sometimes many months or years later. Immediate echolalia can be used as a teaching tool. The echolalic speech phrase can be shaped by using speech rules and by using the echolalic skill to model more appropriate language. For example, when a student echoes back questions, the teacher can shape the response by modeling the appropriate response and reinforcing the use of the appropriate response when the student echoes it. This type of strategy is highly individualized, and it may be appropriate to consult with the speech and language pathologist for specific suggestions for the individual student.

Delayed echolalic utterances may have no obvious meaning for the listener. Students with ASD frequently repeat television commercials word for word. To understand the function of the language behavior, it is helpful to think of it as a chunk of language that has been stored without regard for meaning. A situation or emotion may trigger the use of the words, even if they seem to have no connection to the situation. It is important not to assume that the student understands the content of the echolalic speech being used. When possible, try to determine the situation that has elicited the speech and prompt the appropriate language to use for that situation. For example, when a student echoed the script from a TV cola advertisement, this meant that the student was thirsty. The teacher tested this possibility by verbal prompting with a question such as "You feel thirsty and want a drink?" Sometimes families and teachers never figure out a logical connection for delayed echolalic utterances.

Using Alternative or Augmentative Communication Systems

Many children can benefit from the use of an augmentative communication system. An augmentative communication system is any approach that supports, enhances, or adds to the way a person tells you something. It may be used with both nonverbal students and students who are verbal but appear unable to use speech in a functional way to express wants and needs. Augmentative communication systems can range from low-tech (those not requiring any power source, such as electricity) to high-tech (those systems that require power).

Alternative communication may include the following:

- Directly moving a person or object to communicate (e.g., pulling a teacher to the door when the student wants to go outside)
- Using gestures or body actions to convey meaning (e.g., shaking the head to express negativity)
- Using real objects to convey messages (e.g., bringing a jacket to ask to go home)
- Using picture representations (e.g., the Picture Exchange System, or PECS)
- Using the voice without conventional words (e.g., saying "Ah-ahah" to indicate need for the toilet)
- Using written messages by pointing at already written ones or by writing (e.g., using a word processor to communicate)
- Using sign language gestures from a conventional, nonverbal, formal language (e.g., American Sign Language or Signed English)

Deciding whether to implement an alternative or augmentative communication system and selecting the type of system are both decisions that should be made carefully, based on an assessment of the learner's level of cognitive ability, skills, interests, and motor abilities.

12

Teaching Students With ASD

Strategies for Social Skills

M ost students with ASD would like to be part of the social world around them. They have a need to interact socially and be involved with others. However, one of the defining characteristics of ASD is impairment of social skills. Students with ASD have not automatically learned the rules of interaction with others, and they are unable to follow these unwritten rules of social behavior.

Many people with ASD are operating on false perceptions that are rigid or overly literal. Recognizing these false perceptions can be very helpful in understanding the behavior and needs of these students in social situations. The misperceptions include the following:

- Rules apply in only a single situation.
- Everything someone says must be true.
- When you do not know what to do, do nothing.

Imagine how overly literal misconceptions could seriously limit social interaction. It is a mistake to assume that students with ASD understand any situation or a social expectation. They may be using an ineffective method of interacting because they do not know a more appropriate one, or they may be unable to distinguish between situations to select an appropriate behavior.

Social skill development is an essential curricular area for students with ASD, as well as a crucial component of any intervention plan for changing problem behaviors. To help students, it is necessary to assess their social competencies carefully to determine which social skills must be directly taught.

To develop social skills, students need to have the opportunity to participate and interact in a variety of natural environments where appropriate models, natural cues and stimuli, and functional reinforcers are available. Placement within integrated environments provides this access to peer models and social opportunities. However, access to models and opportunities to develop social skills is not usually enough. In general, people with ASD need explicit teaching to develop social skills and understanding of social situations. There are a variety of promising practices for supporting students with ASD in developing social skills.

Using Social Stories

One of the most helpful methods for teaching social skills is the use of social stories, a strategy developed by Carol Gray. A social story is a description of a social situation that includes the social cues and appropriate responses and that is written for a specific situation for the individual student. The story can be used for a variety of purposes, including the following:

- Facilitating the inclusion of students in regular education classes
- Introducing changes and new routines
- Explaining reasons for the behavior of others
- Teaching situation-specific social skills
- Assisting in teaching new academic skills

Social stories can be created by parents, teachers, and other service providers. They are useful with students who have a level of cognitive functioning that allows them to understand the story. Nonreaders can listen to social stories on cassette tapes. To be effective, a social story should describe a situation from the perspective of the student, direct the student to do the appropriate behavior, and be in the voice of the student (i.e., from the *I* perspective).

The process begins with identifying student needs through observation and assessment. Once a difficult situation is identified, the author observes the situation and tries to understand the perspective of the student in terms of what will be seen, heard, and felt. The author then writes the story at an appropriate comprehension level and from the perspective of the student and includes descriptive, directive, and perspective statements. (Descriptive sentences provide information on the setting, activity, and people involved; directive statements are positive statements about the desired response for a given situation; and perspective statements provide a description of the possible reactions of others.)

There are three basic approaches for implementing a social story:

- For a student who reads independently, the story is read twice by an adult, followed by the student's reading it back. Then the student reads it daily.
- If the student does not read, the story may be recorded on a cassette tape with a signal (e.g., bell) to turn the pages. The student is taught to "read" the story and reads it daily. Symbols, drawings, or photographs can be included in the story to support meaning for the student.
- To incorporate modeling, the story can be videotaped. The story is read aloud on a videotape, with one image on the screen at a time.

Teaching Key Social Rules

Developing an understanding of the basic rules associated with a given situation will help the child to adapt to the social context and may prevent increased anxiety and reduce the reliance on inappropriate coping behaviors. Critical social skills for which students with ASD will likely need some type of direct instruction include these:

- *Waiting.* Visual cues, such as an object, pictures, and written words, can provide concrete information to make waiting less abstract and more specific to the situation.
- *Taking turns.* This can be taught through the use of social stories as well as a picture or pictograph to cue the child. It may also be necessary to provide some instruction and rehearsal in turn-taking activities.

- *Transitions.* Using social stories and providing warnings with visual cues, such as symbols that are understood by the student, can help the student make the transition from one activity to another. Transitions can be particularly difficult if the student has not completed the activity; the student may need to be prepared for the possibility of having to finish later.
- *Changing the topic in conversation.* Some students may stay on one topic and appear unable or unwilling to talk about anything else. Staying with one behavior or topic in this way is referred to as "perseveration." Visual rules, established time limits, and setting a time and place to engage in a favorite topic may help in teaching students when they need to end or change the topic.
- *Finishing.* It may help to teach students to use environmental cues, such as observing and following the behavior of other children. It may also be necessary to use a timer and to teach a method for checking their own work.
- *Initiating.* Social stories combined with photographs or pictures can be particularly useful for teaching a student how to approach others, ask for something, get into a game, say hello, and leave a situation if upset.
- *Being flexible.* Visual systems can be used to explain changes in a concrete way. If sequenced schedules or picture routines are used, a specific picture or symbol can be removed or crossed out and another put in its place.
- *Being quiet.* Visual supports may be helpful in teaching the specific behaviors for being quiet and teaching rules about being quiet or speaking in specific situations.

Using Cognitive Picture Rehearsal

Another instructional strategy for teaching social skills that presents information in a visual format is cognitive picture rehearsal. This method involves presenting a sequence of behaviors in the form of pictures or pictographs with an accompanying script. The student is guided through repeated practice of the sequence of behaviors.

Using Peer Support

Peers can assist students with ASD in developing social skills. It may be helpful to educate the peers first so that they better understand the behavior of the student with ASD. For example, the teacher may need to interpret the nonverbal communication or explain that a specific activity is difficult for the student. Then the teacher can identify what peers can do to help. This can be done informally or in a more structured manner.

Young children can be shown how to use specific prompts to initiate and maintain interaction with a classmate with ASD. They may also need help communicating with the student. Peers should be reinforced for doing their part, just as the student with ASD is reinforced for social interactions.

Peers can be helped to develop strategies to enhance the social competence of the child with ASD. Pivotal response training (PRT) is one technique that has been used successfully during recess breaks to increase interactions, initiation, varied toy play, and language use. PRT involves teaching typical peers to use strategies to do the following:

- Gain attention
- Give choices to maintain motivation
- Vary toys
- Model social behavior
- Reinforce attempts
- Encourage conversation
- Extend conversation
- Take turns
- Narrate play

Students can be provided with information on ASD and tips for interacting with the student with ASD. It is important that parents be involved in the decision to discuss ASD with their child's peers. They may wish to preview any materials or be involved in the presentation.

Using Social Skills Training Groups

Students with ASD may also benefit from social skill instruction within a small-group structured format. A variety of social skills training programs and resources are available. Promising programs include an assessment that is used to identify skills for instruction. Lessons follow a similar format in each of the social skills curricula:

- Identifying the skill and skill components and when it is used
- Modeling the skill
- Role-playing the skill

- Practicing the skill
- Identifying strategies for generalization

Although these curricula are not developed specifically for children with ASD, they can be used in combination with appropriate adaptations and supports. In addition, there may need to be a particular emphasis on the strategies for facilitating generalization of targeted skills.

Integrating Play Groups

Integrated play groups can provide opportunities for younger students with ASD to interact with their age peers and create a natural environment for incidental teaching of social skills. Play groups provide natural situations in which children with ASD use language to express wants, practice being near other children, and imitate social interactions between peers without disabilities.

Teaching Self-Monitoring/Managing Skills

The ultimate goal for all students, including those with ASD, is to increase independent participation in a variety of environments with effective social skills. One way to increase independence in higher-functioning students with ASD is to teach self-management procedures in which students monitor their own behavior to earn positive reinforcement. Studies have shown that in the process of the students collecting their own self-monitoring data, the desired behavior increases. The accuracy of the self-monitoring may not be as important as the process and awareness it builds in the student.

The process for teaching self-management is as follows:

1. Define the target behavior that the student will self-monitor.

2. Identify reinforcers that function successfully for the individual.

3. Create a self-monitoring method for the student to collect data (e.g., a chart, stickers, or some kind of low-tech counter device).

4. Teach the student the target behavior and how to use the self-monitoring method to record the performance of the behavior.

5. Increase the student's independence by gradually reducing adult intervention and having the student self-manage behavior.

Supporting the Development of Friendships

Optimally, the aim of developing specific social skills is to enable the student to interact with others in a variety of settings and to facilitate the development of social opportunities and relationships. Students who demonstrate basic social skills may still have difficulty establishing connections with other children and maintaining interactions with peers. Teachers and parents may facilitate further social interaction in the following ways:

- Encouraging a friend to play with the child at home
- Helping the student join school clubs, with support as needed to participate
- Teaching the child to observe other children and imitate them
- Encouraging cooperative games
- Modeling how to relate to the child and educating other students in the class to do the same
- Encouraging prospective friendships
- Providing enjoyment at break times
- Doing projects and activities that illustrate the qualities of a good friend
- Helping the student to understand emotions through direct teaching of how to read people's faces and body language and respond to cues that indicate different emotions

13

Children With Asperger Syndrome

Characteristics, Learning Styles, and Intervention Strategies

Asperger syndrome (AS) was named for a Viennese psychiatrist, Hans Asperger. In 1944, Asperger published a paper in German describing a consistent pattern of abilities and behaviors that occurred primarily in boys. In the early 1980s, Asperger's paper was translated into English, which resulted in international recognition for his work in this area.

In the 1990s, specific diagnostic criteria for AS were included in the American Psychiatric Association's *Diagnostic and Statistical Manual of Mental Disorders*, 4th edition (*DSM-IV*) as well as the *International Classification of Diseases*, 10th edition (*ICD10*). In general, *DSM-IV* and *ICD10* base their diagnostic criteria for Asperger syndrome on the

Material from this chapter appears courtesy of Susan Stokes under a contract with CESA 7 and funded by a discretionary grant from the Wisconsin Department of Public Instruction. *Children With Asperger Syndrome Characteristics/Learning Styles and Intervention Strategies.* Retrieved on August 30, 2007 from http://www.bbbautism .com/pdf/article_64_children_with_Aspergers.pdf. Used with permission.

following (American Psychiatric Association, 1994; World Health Organization, 1990):

- Impairment of social interaction
- Impairment of social communication
- Impairment of social imagination, flexible thinking, and imaginative play
- Absence of a significant delay in cognitive development
- Absence of general delay in language development (In Wisconsin, the child may still have an impairment under the state's eligibility criteria for speech and language.)

Recent research establishes the prevalence of Asperger syndrome as approximately 1 in 300, affecting boys to girls at a ratio of 10:1. Children with clinical (medical) diagnoses of Asperger syndrome who have been identified by schools as "children with disabilities" are typically found by the IEP team conducting the evaluation to have an impairment in such areas as autism, speech/language, or other health impaired. Depending on the unique characteristics of the child, other impairment areas listed under state law for special education may also be considered and used.

The general features and characteristics exhibited by children diagnosed with Asperger syndrome are similar to the general features and characteristics exhibited by children who have been clinically diagnosed with ASD and are described as having "high-functioning autism." For educational purposes, the remainder of this paper focuses on the child with Asperger syndrome who has been identified by the IEP team as being a child with a disability. Much of the following information is also relevant for working with children identified as having ASD who are described as having "high-functioning autism."

Training

Each person who comes in contact with a child diagnosed with Asperger syndrome (either school staff or peers) should receive training on the unique characteristics and educational needs of such children. Due to confidentiality issues, this training should always be discussed first with the parents of the child with Asperger syndrome, and their written consent should be obtained prior to providing peer training.

Educational staff training should include the following two components:

- *General training of the entire school staff.* Prior to working with children with Asperger syndrome, it is critical to understand the unique features and characteristics of this developmental disability. Staff should be informed that children with Asperger syndrome have a developmental disability that causes them to respond and behave in a way that is different from other students. Most importantly, the responses/behaviors exhibited by these children should not be misinterpreted as purposeful and manipulative behaviors.

- *Child-specific training for educational staff who will be working directly with the child.* Educational staff who will be working directly with children with Asperger syndrome should understand each child's individual strengths and needs prior to working with them. A team of persons familiar with the child and his or her disability should provide this training. The team may include previous teacher(s), speech/language pathologist, occupational therapist, teacher's aide, and most importantly, the child's parents.

Characteristics and Learning Styles: General

The following characteristics and learning styles associated with Asperger syndrome are important to consider when planning an appropriate educational program for the child, particularly their impact on learning. Children with Asperger syndrome exhibit difficulty in appropriately processing incoming information. The brain's ability to take in, store, and use information is significantly different from that of neuro-typically developing children. This results in a somewhat unusual perspective on the world. Therefore, teaching strategies for children with Asperger syndrome will be different than strategies used for neuro-typically developing children.

Children with Asperger syndrome typically exhibit strengths in their visual processing skills while having significant weaknesses in their ability to process auditory information. Therefore, use of visual methods of teaching, as well as visual support strategies, should always be incorporated to help the child with Asperger syndrome better understand the environment.

The remainder of this chapter describes ten primary characteristics of children with Asperger syndrome and intervention strategies for each.

1. Social Relation Difficulties

Characteristics

Children with Asperger syndrome tend to exhibit a lack of *effectiveness* in social interactions rather than a lack of social interactions.

They tend to have difficulty knowing how to "make connections" socially. Social situations are easily misread by children with Asperger syndrome, and as a result, their interactions and responses are often interpreted by others as being odd.

Children with Asperger syndrome can exhibit low self-esteem and possible depression, particularly when they reach adolescence, due to their painful awareness of the social differences that exist between them and their peers. They have a desire to "fit in" socially yet have no idea how to do this. Children with Asperger syndrome can be significantly impacted by the following characteristics of social relations.

Social Reciprocity

Children with Asperger syndrome can exhibit an imbalance in reciprocal social relations (i.e., the give-and-take in social relationships), which can be exhibited in several ways:

- *Recognizing and interpreting various social situations.* Typically developing children are able to recognize and interpret the social nuances of various social situations without being specifically taught. Their intact processing systems allow for this to occur. However, children with Asperger syndrome typically have great difficulty recognizing, understanding, and thus applying appropriate social skills to various social situations. Their distinctive processing/learning systems do not readily allow for accurate recognition and interpretation of this seemingly abstract information.
- *Social rules.* Children with Asperger syndrome typically do not learn social rules, either by observing others or through frequent verbal reminders. These children do not appear to be intentionally ignoring and/or breaking these rules. Instead, they have a difficult time accurately perceiving social environments, and, thus, they do not understand that a particular social rule is to be applied in a specific social context.

Example: A teacher frequently reminds a child with Asperger syndrome, prior to going out for recess, that he cannot push other children. The child repeats this rule prior to going out to recess. However, when the child goes onto the playground at recess, he pushes several children.

- *Friendship skills.* Children with Asperger syndrome tend to exhibit limited knowledge of the concept of friendship.

> **Example:** When a teenager with Asperger syndrome was asked if he had any friends, he responded that friendship was an area where he had some problems. He was able to name two peers whom he considered "friends"; however, he did not know the last name of one of the students. He proceeded to describe the student to see if the listener knew the student's last name. When asked why these students were his friends, he said because he saw them in the hallway during passing period and that he also saw one of the students at a weekly church youth group meeting. When asked if he and his "friends" went to each other's houses, talked on the phone, etc., the teen with Asperger syndrome said no, that he just saw them at different places.

- *Children with Asperger syndrome also do not appear to attend to or respond to peer pressure.* They may have definite preferences for clothing to achieve a comfort level in relation to their sensory sensitivities without regard or concern for popular styles as worn by peers.

> **Example:** Some children prefer no ridges on the collar, no buttons down the front of a shirt, no blue jeans—only elastic-waist pants, no long/short sleeves or long/short pants, etc.

- *Understanding and expressing varied emotional states.* Children with Asperger syndrome may have difficulty identifying (labeling and understanding) varied emotional states, both in themselves and in others. In addition, regulation of emotional states can be extremely difficult.

> **Example:** When experiencing great distress, a child with Asperger syndrome continually asks others for monitoring of his emotional state: "Am I under control yet?" He has limited awareness of when he is calm versus extremely upset. Another example would be laughing, seemingly inappropriately, when others are hurt, embarrassed, etc. One child with Asperger's syndrome physically manipulates his face when requested to exhibit various emotional states.

Social Relationships: Intervention Strategies

The child with Asperger syndrome will need to be directly taught various social skills (recognition, comprehension, and application) in one-to-one and/or small-group settings. Social skills training will also be needed to generalize previously learned social skills from highly structured, supportive contexts to less-structured settings and, eventually, real-life situations. It is important to emphasize that children with Asperger syndrome will not learn social relations by watching other people or by participating in various social situations. They tend to have great difficulty even recognizing the essential information of a social situation, let alone processing/interpreting it appropriately.

Tools for Teaching Social Skills

- The use of social stories and social scripts can provide children with visual information and strategies that will improve their understanding of various social situations. In addition, the social stories/scripts can teach children appropriate behaviors to exhibit when they are engaged in varied social situations. The repetitious "reading" of the social story/script makes this strategy effective for the child with Asperger syndrome.
- Role-playing various social situations can be an effective tool for teaching a child appropriate social responses.
- Videotaping/audiotaping both appropriate and inappropriate social behaviors can assist the child in learning to identify and respond appropriately to various social situations.
- "Lunch/recess club" is a structured lunch/recess time with specific peers in which the child with Asperger syndrome can focus on developing target social skills. This strategy can assist in generalizing social skills previously learned in a structured setting.
- Comic strip conversations can be used to clarify social interactions and emotional relations visually.

- Peer partners/buddies: Specific peer(s) can be chosen to accompany and possibly assist the child with Asperger syndrome during less-structured social situations and when experiencing social difficulties (e.g., out-of-class transitions, recess, lunch, etc.). This peer support network should initially be established in a small-group setting.

- Individualized visual social "rule" cards can be taped to the child's desk as a visual reminder regarding appropriate social behaviors to exhibit. Portable rule cards can be used for environments other than the classroom. The rules can be written on index cards, laminated, and then given to the child to carry along as visual reminders of the social rules for any particular context.

2. Social Communication Difficulties

Characteristics

The child with Asperger syndrome typically exhibits highly articulate and verbose expressive language skills with a large vocabulary, particularly regarding specific topics (high interest areas). However, his or her convincing language skills can easily be misinterpreted as advanced communication skills. In turn, this can result in a mislabeling the child's actions as purposeful or manipulative rather than as behavior that is due to the child's significant difficulty in understanding and using appropriate social communication skills. Children with Asperger syndrome often lack social communication skills to sustain even minimal social communicative interactions in any of the following areas:

- *Conversational discourse skills.* Children with Asperger syndrome can generally engage in routine social interactions, such as greetings. However, they may exhibit significant difficulty engaging in extended interactions or two-way relationships. They can have difficulty initiating and maintaining appropriate conversations, engaging in conversational turn taking, and changing topics in an appropriate manner. Their language can be extremely egocentric in that they tend to talk at people instead of with them, resulting in one-sided conversations. Incessant question asking can also be prevalent, as well as difficulty in repairing conversational breakdowns.
- *Understanding and using nonverbal social communication (discourse) skills.* Children with Asperger syndrome can have significant difficulty interpreting nonverbal social communication skills used to regulate social interactions (e.g., tone of voice, facial expressions, body postures, gestures, personal space,

vocal volume, use of eye contact to "read" faces, etc.). For example, they may not understand that a raised voice can convey an emotional state such as anger. (In one case, a student with Asperger syndrome stated, "Why are you talking louder? I can hear you," when his mother raised her voice to communicate anger.) These children may also have difficulty interpreting nonverbal cues that the listener might be giving to communicate that a conversational breakdown has occurred (e.g., facial expressions to indicate not understanding the message, boredom, etc.). Some children with Asperger syndrome can exhibit conversational speech with a somewhat flat affect (i.e., limited change in vocal tone, volume, pitch, stress, and rhythm), particularly to indicate emotion and/or emphasize key words.

- *Narrative discourse skills.* Children with Asperger syndrome can exhibit difficulty with their narrative discourse skills, including relating past events or retelling movies, stories, and television shows in a cohesive and sequential manner. They may leave out important pieces of relational information, as well as referents, and they may use many revisions, pauses, and/or repetitions.

> **Example:** A child with Asperger syndrome was relating his weekend to the class. The child with Asperger syndrome said: "Back through time, uhm, uhm, at my Grandma's, uh, it was [pause] back through time. I was, I was, I [pause] I uh, a long time ago. I was at my Grandma's."

Social Communication: Target Skills and Strategies for Intervention

The following social communication skills (pragmatic language skills) may be focused on for direct instruction, depending upon the child's individualized needs:

- Initiation of appropriate social interactions for various situations through appropriate verbal utterances, rather than actions or behaviors. For example, on the playground, the child with Asperger syndrome should use the words "Wanna play chase?" to ask a peer to play tag, rather than going up to the peer and shoving her.
- Initiation in conversation of varied topics, not only topics related to high-interest areas

- Topic maintenance in conversation, particularly of topics initiated by others
- Conversational turn taking across 3–4 turns (reciprocal communication skills)
- Asking questions of others related to topics initiated by others
- Calling attention to communicative utterances. Children direct their communication to others by first calling other people's attention to themselves.
- Comprehension and use of nonverbal social communication skills: tone of voice, personal space, vocal volume, body orientation, facial expressions, etc.
- Narrative discourse skills: relating past events and retelling stories sequentially and cohesively by including important pieces of relational information as well as referents
- Greeting others
- Seeking assistance appropriately (e.g., raising hand for help in the classroom)

3. Language Comprehension/ Auditory Processing Difficulties

Characteristics

Children with Asperger syndrome generally interpret auditory information literally and concretely. They can have difficulty understanding figurative language, including jokes/riddles, words with multiple meanings, teasing, and implied meanings.

Example 1: A child with Asperger syndrome was participating in a local basketball clinic. He was playing very well, and the coach made the comment, "Wow! Your mom must have put gas in your shoes this morning." The child quickly looked at his mother with a worried expression. His mother shook her head no and encouraged him to keep on playing. The child responded to the coach, "Not today."

Example 2: A mother said to her child, "Stop back-talking to me." The child said, "I'm sorry Mom, I'll talk to your front."

It is also important to note that delays in processing auditory information may be present in children with Asperger syndrome. Even though they may be able to comprehend the auditory information, they may need additional time to process this information prior to responding. They may also have difficulty following multistep auditory directions (e.g., "Go back to your desk and take out your journals, then write about your weekend.").

Language Comprehension/Auditory Processing: Intervention Strategies

- Auditory information/prompting should be kept to a minimum, as it can be too overwhelming for some children. Visual cues should be used to assist the child to more readily comprehend directions, questions, rules, figurative language, etc.
- Give the child with Asperger syndrome enough time to respond, to allow for possible auditory processing difficulties, before repeating/rephrasing the question/directive. Children can be taught appropriate phrases to indicate they need additional processing time (e.g., "Give me a minute—I'm thinking.").
- Written rules can help the children understand what is expected of them at all times. Reference to the rules can be used rather than verbally telling them what to do or what not to do.
- Auditory directions can be written on a dry-erase board for children with Asperger syndrome, greatly increasing their ability to complete tasks/activities independently.
- The adults in the child's environment should be aware of the child's concrete/literal interpretation of figurative language and should provide concrete explanations if necessary. Focus should also be given to increasing the child's comprehension of figurative language skills, such as idioms, words with multiple meanings, jokes, teasing, etc., through the use of visual supports.

4. Sensory Processing Difficulties

Characteristics

The child with Asperger syndrome may exhibit some sensory processing difficulties that result in atypical responses to sensory input (auditory, visual, tactile, smell, taste, and movement). This difficulty in organizing the child's sensory input, experiencing both hypersensitive responses (overresponses) and hyposensitive responses (underresponses) to various sensory stimuli, can cause him or her to experience stress and anxiety when trying to interpret the environment accurately. Sensory processing difficulties can also markedly decrease the child's ability to sustain focused attention. It is important to note that the processing of sensory information can be extremely inconsistent; that is, at one time, the child may experience a hypersensitive response to a specific sensory stimuli but at another time may exhibit a typical or a hyposensitive response.

> **Example 1:** A child with Asperger syndrome was eating in a restaurant with family members and experiencing sensory overload. He ate as quickly as possible and then asked if he could go outside. The child paced for 20 minutes back and forth in front of the restaurant while waiting for the rest of the family to finish eating. While riding home, he pulled the hood of his coat all the way over his face and tied it tightly to try to block out all sensory stimuli.
>
> **Example 2:** While watching television with his family, a child with Asperger syndrome put his hands over his ears and exclaimed "That TV is driving me crazy!"
>
> **Example 3:** A child with Asperger syndrome exhibited an extreme sensory sensitivity to the sight and smell of eggs, particularly hard-boiled eggs. The child gagged and vomited when exposed to hard-boiled eggs.

Sensory Processing: Intervention Strategies

It is important to be aware of possible auditory sensitivities and how the environment might be contributing to the child's marked increase in anxiety and challenging behaviors. Strategies to accommodate for auditory sensitivities can include the following:

- Use headphones/headband to muffle extraneous auditory stimuli.
- Use headphones to listen to calming music, when appropriate.
- Forewarn children of any fire drills, tornado drills, etc. This can be done both verbally and visually (on their schedules). Although children may appear calm outwardly, as though readily handling this change in routine, they may be experiencing internal stress/anxiety, which could appear later.
- Use a daily sensory diet, consisting of access to various sensory-calming activities and/or physical activities (as deemed necessary), which are scheduled throughout the child's day. This can decrease the child's stress, anxiety, and repetitive behaviors as well as increase his or her calm/relaxed states and focused

attention. Sensory "break" activities should be visually represented on the child's daily schedule.

- Incorporating heavy work patterns (e.g., push, pull, carry) into functional tasks/jobs appears to assist some children in becoming more calm and focused. Examples might include taking the attendance or lunch room count to the office for each classroom, getting the milk cartons for the kindergarten classrooms and delivering them to each classroom, sweeping a walkway, carrying books back to the library, cleaning the chalkboard, etc.

- Using a "quiet space/area" to decrease sensory overload and increase self-calming is another strategy. The quiet space should be a specified location/area with objects that are calming to the child (e.g., Koosh balls, books, beanbag chair). For children who transition to various classrooms, the use of a "home base" classroom as a safe place to go is suggested when they feel the need for calming. Access to a "fiddle basket," containing small items for the children to manipulate (e.g., small Koosh balls, clothespins, etc.) can help calm the children and focus their attention at certain times during the day (e.g., while sitting and listening to a story read aloud by the teacher).

- To avoid sensory overload during transitions such as changing class periods, going to/from recess, or changing clothes for gym in the locker room, allow the child to transition a few minutes earlier or later than the rest of the students.

5. Difficulty Representing Language Internally

Characteristics

Children with Asperger syndrome can "blurt out" their thoughts as statements of factual information, resulting in an appearance of insensitivity and lack of tact. These children typically do not understand that some thoughts and ideas can and should be represented internally and, thus, should not be spoken aloud. Therefore, whatever they think, they tend to say aloud.

Example 1: "Mrs. Jones, why are you wearing that dress? It looks just like a bathrobe."

Example 2: "This is boring. Don't you think this is boring, Ryan?"

Typically developing children can internalize thoughts by the time they are 5 to 6 years old. This aspect of language should show improvement as the child learns how to take the perspective of others. This perspective-taking ability is sometimes referred to being able to "mind read" or developing "theory of mind."

Representing Language Internally: Intervention Strategies

- Initially, encourage the child to whisper, rather than speak his thoughts aloud. Next, encourage him to "think it—don't say it."
- Role-playing, audio/videotaping, and social scripting can all be used to teach the child how to identify what thoughts should be represented internally, not aloud. Role-playing will allow the child to practice this skill.

6. Insistence on Sameness

Characteristics

Children with Asperger syndrome can be easily overwhelmed by minimal changes in routines and can exhibit a definite preference for rituals. As a result, these children can become quite anxious and worry incessantly about the unknown; that is, when the environment becomes unpredictable and they do not know what to expect.

> **Example:** Unpredictability may occur during less-structured activities or times of the day: recess, lunch, free play or other free time, physical education, bus rides to/from school, music class, art class, assemblies, field trips, substitute teachers, delayed start/early dismissal, etc.

The following features are important to consider for the child with Asperger syndrome:

- *Rigid, egocentric perceptions:* Children with Asperger syndrome tend to have very rigid, egocentric perceptions of the world and, thus, can become quite upset when changes occur that "go against" their preconceived "rules" or perceptions. Therefore, when a new situation occurs, they have to learn a "new rule" (perception), which can be very upsetting to them (e.g., indoor recess due to inclement weather).

- *Strict adherence to rules:* Children with Asperger syndrome may generate rules based upon their perceptions of various experiences. As a result, they may adhere strictly to these self-imposed rules and expect others to do so as well. When these rules are "broken" by others, this can create a great deal of stress/anxiety in children with Asperger syndrome.

> **Example:** Whenever a particular child with Asperger syndrome tells someone, "Thank you," he expects the person to respond immediately with, "You're welcome." If the person does not immediately respond, the child will perseverate in saying, "Thank you," and become increasingly anxious until the person says, "You're welcome."

- Conversely, when given rules by others (teachers, parents, etc.), children with Asperger syndrome tend to interpret these rules strictly and concretely, as well as value strict adherence to the rule—for both themselves and others.

> **Example:** A child with Asperger syndrome was given the following rules in art class by the teacher regarding markers: no throwing markers, no chewing on the markers, no smashing marker tips. The child with Asperger syndrome imitated a peer and connected the markers together to make a long, sword-type structure. This child and the peer engaged in a "sword fight." Both children got in trouble for this behavior, although the child with Asperger syndrome was truly confused as to why he was in trouble because he hadn't broken any rules, according to his perceptions.

- *Need for closure/completion:* In relation to their ritualistic needs, children with Asperger syndrome can exhibit an intense need for closure or completion of a task or activity before transitioning to the next. This can create significant educational implications if not planned for accordingly. For example, if a math worksheet cannot be completed prior to recess, children with Asperger syndrome may become quite upset—even though they may enjoy going outside for recess very much. The anxiety relates to the need for closure, a ritualistic need, rather than in relation to the specific activities at hand, and it typically cannot be alleviated by being told that the activity can completed later.

Insistence on Sameness: Intervention Strategies

- It is important to provide a consistent, predictable environment with minimal transitions.
- Use of a visual schedule can provide children with information relating to their day, as well as preparing them for any changes that might occur in their daily routine.
- Visual and auditory forewarning/foreshadowing are critical, to give the child much-needed information relating to possible changes in routines.
- Assignments may need to be modified so that the child can complete them within a specific amount of time, prior to transitioning to the next activity.
- Use of a "finish later" folder or box may be helpful. Even though children may be reminded verbally that they can finish their math worksheet after recess, this information will not be processed as readily as if communicated with a visual strategy.

7. Poor Concentration, Distractibility, and Disorganization

Characteristics

Children with Asperger syndrome can often appear off-task and may be easily distracted by both internal stimuli (perseverative thoughts/concerns) and external stimuli (sensory input). For example, a child sees a single cloud in the sky and begins to obsess about whether it is going to rain and/or possibly storm (internal stimulus distraction). Or the child attends to a fly buzzing around the room, or a flickering fluorescent light, rather than the teacher (external stimulus distraction). Screening out information that is irrelevant can be very difficult, requiring conscious effort by the child with Asperger syndrome.

In addition, children with Asperger syndrome can exhibit significant difficulties regarding both their internal and external organizational skills, including the following:

- *Organizing their thoughts and ideas to express themselves in a cohesive manner.* For example, a child with Asperger syndrome was asked to explain how he figured out the answer to the math problem, $900 \times 3 = 2,700$. He responded: "Well, first of all, $9 \times 3 = 27$ and $90 \times 3 = 270$ and $900 \times 3 = 2,700$, and it sort of reminds me of another kind of math problem like the other day when you're multiplying and, uh, it goes 9 × 3 = 27 and then, uhm, its like . . . I don't really know what I'm saying."

- *Gathering educational materials needed for specific tasks or activities, such as homework.*
- *Keeping track of their belongings.* These include personal and educational materials, such as assignments.
- *Organizing their desks, lockers, etc.*

Concentration, Distractibility, and Disorganization: Intervention Strategies

- A highly structured educational environment may be indicated for the child with Asperger syndrome to experience success.
- Use of a timer (e.g., an egg timer) provides time constraints and structure for completing tasks. When given an unlimited amount of time, children with Asperger syndrome may take an unlimited amount of time for task completion. However, caution should be taken in using timers. Some children may become highly interested in (thus, distracted by) the amount of time that is passing, via the timer, thereby becoming less attentive to completing the task. Other children have exhibited extreme anxiety when timers are used because they become overly focused on the amount of time passing, perceiving that they cannot complete the task within the time constraint given.
- A written (visual) checklist is used to keep children focused and on-task so that they can complete each step listed in sequential order. This visual tool (e.g., a "morning routine" checklist or "homework" checklist) allows for independent completion of an entire routine or task.
- A daily (individualized) visual schedule should be used to communicate to the children what is currently happening, when they are "all done" with something, what is coming up next, and any changes that might occur. (Please refer to the section on structured teaching in Chapter 5 for more information regarding visual schedules.)
- Use of a visual calendar both at home and at school will give the child information regarding upcoming events/activities. When children ask when a particular event (e.g., class field trip, bath night, swimming lessons, etc.) will occur, they easily can be referred to the calendar, which presents the information through the more readily understood visual mode.

- Give written directions or cues whenever possible in various contexts/environments. Small dry-erase boards and index cards are good tools to use for written directions, as they are easily portable. For example, in computer lab, a three-step direction could be written down to give children information as to what they need to do independently, rather than giving them continual auditory prompting for completion of the task.
- Use color-coded notebooks to match academic books.
- Use an assignment notebook consistently.
- Worksheets may need to be reorganized. Modifications could include fewer problems per sheet; larger, highly visual space for responding; and boxes next to each question to be checked when completed.
- For class lectures, peer buddies may be needed to take notes. No-carbon-required (NCR) paper can be used, or the student's notes could be copied on a copy machine.
- Use of an "Assignments to Be Completed" folder, as well as a "Completed Assignments" folder, is also recommended.

8. Emotional Vulnerability

Characteristics

Children with Asperger syndrome often have the intellectual ability to participate successfully in the regular education curriculum. However, they may lack the social and emotional abilities to cope with the demands of the regular education environment, such as regular classroom, recess, and lunch. As a result, these children may exhibit low self-esteem, may be self-critical, and may be unable to tolerate making mistakes (perfectionist). Thus, they can become easily overwhelmed, stressed, and frustrated, resulting in behavioral outbursts due to poor coping strategies/self-regulation. These children can appear quite anxious for most of their waking day as they continually attempt to manage an ever-changing, sensory-overstimulating, social world.

Emotional Vulnerability: Intervention Strategies

- Utilize the child's strength areas and incorporate them into special projects or assignments for the child to present to the class. This activity may increase the child's self-esteem with peers. For example, a child with a high interest in geography could give a presentation to the class relating geography to the current area of study.

- Teach children relaxation techniques that they could learn to implement on their own to decrease anxiety levels (e.g., "Take a big breath, count to ten.") These steps could initially be written down as visual cue cards for children to carry and refer to as needed.

9. Restricted/Perseverative Range of Interests

Characteristics

Children with Asperger syndrome tend to have eccentric preoccupations or odd, intense fixations, as noted by the following behaviors:

- Relentless "lectures" on a specific areas of interest
- Repetitive questions about interests, concerns, or worries
- Trouble "letting go" of thoughts or ideas, particularly relating to concerns or worries
- Refusal to learn about anything outside of a limited field of interest, as they do not appear to understand the significance of other information.

Common high-interest areas for many children with Asperger syndrome may include the *Wheel of Fortune* game show, transportation, astronomy, animals, dinosaurs, geography, weather, and maps. It is important to note that perseverative behaviors can often resemble obsessive-compulsive behaviors.

> **Example:** Perfectionism regarding written work may mean the child erases the same printed letter numerous times in succession due to the seemingly imperfect quality of the letter formation, resulting in increased frustration/anxiety. One child with Asperger syndrome exhibits a high interest in Barbie dolls. She cannot go to bed unless all of her Barbies are lined up in the exact same way.

Restricted/Perseverative Range of Interests: Intervention Strategies

- Set aside specific times of the day, and specific time periods, for children to discuss their strong interests. This "discussion time" can even be included on their visual schedules. If the children bring up a perseverative topic/question at another time, refer them to their visual schedule to indicate when they can converse about this topic.

- Provide a written answer to repetitive questions asked by children. When children repeat the question, they can be referred to the written answers, which may assist in comprehension and thus decrease the occurrence of the repetitive question asking.
- Incorporate the children's strong interests into academics (e.g., if a child has a high interest in maps, use maps to teach math skills). With creativity and individualization, almost any high-interest area can be infused into any academic area. Many students with Asperger syndrome have sustained their high interests into higher educational studies and subsequent vocations. For example, Temple Grandin holds a PhD in animal sciences and has designed over one-third of our country's animal livestock holding facilities.

10. Difficulty Taking the Perspective of Others (Mind Reading/Theory of Mind Deficit)

Characteristics

Children with Asperger syndrome can have great difficulty understanding that other people can have thoughts, intentions, needs, desires, and beliefs different from their own. Thus, their perceptions of the world are often viewed as rigid and egocentric, when in reality, they are simply unable to infer other people's mental states. Typically developing children acquire "theory of mind" skills by age 4, yet it estimated that this concept develops between the ages of 9–14 in children with Asperger syndrome. The following are educational implications for children who have theory of mind deficit:

- When the teacher poses a question to the class, the child thinks that the teacher is speaking directly (and only) to him or her and, therefore, calls out the answer.
- Children with Asperger syndrome can be extremely vulnerable to wrongful intent initiated by other children. They can have great difficulty reading the intentions of others and understanding the motives behind their behavior. For example, a fifth-grade student "befriended" a child with Asperger syndrome and told him to say and do many inappropriate behaviors, for which he got into trouble.
- Due to difficulty in understanding the emotional perspective of others, the child may exhibit a seeming lack of empathy. For

example, a child with Asperger syndrome may laugh inappropriately when another child gets hurt.

- Children with Asperger syndrome may have difficulty understanding that their behavior (both actions and words) can affect how others think or feel. They don't appear to understand that their words or actions can make someone feel different from their own emotional state. They are not purposefully trying to hurt others. They are factually relating information without regard to the other person's feelings.

Example 1: If the child with Asperger syndrome wants to play on the computer during free time, he may attempt to do so with little or no regard for the child who is already using the computer.

Example 2: The child with Asperger syndrome may state quite bluntly, "Someone stinks in here. I think it's Lori. Lori, you stink!"

- Cooperative learning groups can be extremely challenging for children with Asperger syndrome. Again, they may have difficulty understanding that the other children in their group can have thoughts and ideas different from their own. This can often result in a significant increase in the child's stress, frustration, and anxiety, leading to the possible occurrence of challenging behaviors.
- Children may have difficulty taking into account what other people know or can be expected to know, leading to confusion on the part of the listener.

Mind Reading/Theory of Mind Deficit: Intervention Strategies

- Training designed specifically to address the above issues will assist the child in learning to consider the perspectives of others. *Teaching Children With Autism to Mind-Read: A Practical Guide* is a good resource book with specific skills and activities clearly outlined for intervention (Howlin, Baron-Cohen, & Hadwin, 1998).
- Children will need to be taught to recognize the effect of their actions on others. If they something offensive, let them know very concretely and literally that "words hurt, just like getting punched in the arm." Encourage children to stop and think how a person will feel before they act or speak.

- Comic strip conversations can be used as a tool to clarify communicative social interactions and emotional relations visually through the use of simple line drawings. Specific colors are used to convey various emotional states for both the speaker and listener.
- Children's literature, videos, movies, or television shows can be used to teach children to interpret the actions of the characters, thus teaching them how to figure out what other people know.

Conclusion

Children with Asperger syndrome exhibit significant social communicative difficulties, as well as other defining characteristics, which may severely impact their ability to function successfully in all facets of life. However, when given appropriate support strategies, through direct teaching and various accommodations and/or modifications, the child with Asperger syndrome can learn to be successful in our unpredictable, sensory-overloading, socially interactive world. It is critical that a team approach be utilized in addressing the unique and challenging needs of a child with Asperger syndrome, with parents being vital members of this team.

14

Assistive Technology for Children With ASD

For years, different modes of technology have been used to improve the quality of life of people with various developmental disabilities. However, the varied use of technology for children with ASD continues to receive limited attention, despite the fact that technology tends to be a high-interest area for many of these children.

This chapter will discuss how various modes of technology, including technology designed as an augmentative communication system, can be used for children with ASD to increase or improve their skills in the following areas:

- Overall understanding of their environment
- Expressive communication skills
- Social interaction skills
- Attention skills
- Motivation skills
- Organization skills
- Academic skills
- Overall independent daily functioning skills

Material from this chapter appears courtesy of Susan Stokes under a contract with CESA 7 and funded by a discretionary grant from the Wisconsin Department of Public Instruction. *Assistive Technology for Children With ASD*. Retrieved on August 30, 2007 from http://www.specialed.us/autism/assist/asst10.htm. Used with permission.

What Is Assistive Technology?

According to the Technology-Related Assistance for Individuals with Disabilities Act of 1988, an *assistive technology* means any item, piece of equipment, or product system, whether acquired commercially or off the shelf and whether modified or customized, that is used to increase, maintain, or improve functional capabilities of individuals with disabilities. *Assistive technology service* is any service that directly assists an individual with a disability in the selection, acquisition, or use of an assistive technology device.

Typically, children with autism process visual information more easily than auditory information. Anytime we use assistive technology devices with these children, we're giving them information through their strongest processing area (visual). Therefore, various types of technology, from low-tech to high-tech, should be incorporated into every aspect of daily living to improve the functional capabilities of children with autism.

Visual Representation Systems

It is important to determine which visual representation system is best understood by the child and in what contexts. Various visual systems, such as objects, photographs, realistic drawings, line drawings, and written words, can be used with assorted modes of technology, as long as the child can readily comprehend the visual representation.

Some children may need different visual representation systems in different situations. This may depend upon numerous factors, such as the skill being taught, as well as the unique characteristics of autism: attending, organization, distractibility, etc.

> **Example:** A child may use real objects for his visual schedule, as the objects appear to give him more information as to where he's going and what's coming up next, as well as to help him remain more focused during the transition. However, this same child may use photographs or line drawings in a picture exchange to communicate expressively.

Some researchers suggest that, for most children, it is best to start with a visual representation system of line drawings and move to a more concrete representation system of photographs or objects as needed.

The Mayer-Johnson software program, Boardmaker, is a user-friendly program for both adults and children. The program offers a 3,000 picture communication symbol (PCS) library in either black-and-white or color, and each PCS can be accompanied by any written word/message. The symbols can be made in any size and tend to be universally understood. They present a relatively clear, uncluttered representation and remove any ambiguity, which can sometimes arise when using photographs, especially personally made photographs.

Example: A teacher took photographs of the various teachers that a child with ASD encountered at school to help him learn the names of his teachers. When reviewing the names of the teachers in the photographs, the child referred to the photograph of a particular teacher as "Mexico." Upon further review of this photo, the teacher realized that in the background, barely visible, was the corner of a map of Mexico. Although the teacher's face was the prominent feature in the photo, the child processed the minimally visible map as the most prominent feature and labeled the photograph accordingly.

When using line drawings, such as those in Boardmaker, caution should also be used when determining whether to use black-and-white or color picture communication symbols. Some children with ASD may prefer or dislike specific colors, and they may focus only on the color instead of processing the entire picture. This will render the PCS virtually meaningless to the children, as they are not processing the entire picture. Black-and-white picture communication symbols tend to remove any ambiguity that might arise.

Example: If a child prefers the color red, and the picture communication symbol (PCS) for *lunch* has a red apple as well as a brown sandwich and orange juice, the child may only process the apple, as it contains her preferred color. The child may not even process the image but attend only to the color red. Therefore, the PCS becomes nonmeaningful to the child.

If the child has difficulty understanding the PCS line drawings and needs a more concrete representation, a good software program to use is Picture This. This program allows for the presentation of real photos without risking ambiguous background clutter, which can be a part of personal photographs. Picture This contains over 2,700 photos from numerous categories that are ideal for

- Creating schedules;
- Augmentative communication systems;
- Games;
- Reading activities;
- Sequence activities for following directions; and
- Various academic activities.

> **Strategy:** To teach a child who is using photographs or objects as his visual representation system to understand black-and-white line drawings, place a small black-and-white picture communication symbol in the corner of the various objects/photographs currently used by the child. Gradually increase the size of the picture communication symbol until it eventually covers up the entire photograph/object.

For children who have difficulty understanding two-dimensional visual representation systems (e.g., photos, drawings, line drawings) and require objects as their visual representation systems, the use of true object-based icons (TOBIs) is suggested. These TOBIs can be any line drawing, picture, etc., that is cut out in the actual shape or outline of the item it represents. Children can both see and feel the symbol and shape, thus assisting them to more readily understand the two-dimensional representation system. TOBIs tend to be somewhat larger than the typical two-dimensional visual representation system. When first introduced, they may be three inches across or larger. The printed word label should always accompany the picture and should be placed strategically so as not to alter the symbol shape.

> **Strategy:** When any visual representation system is used, it is important to combine it with a written word, as many children with ASD exhibit a high interest in letters and words, and some even become early readers. Therefore, we should continually enhance the child's literacy skills by providing the written word with any type of visual representation system.

The rest of this chapter will outline the various skill areas commonly associated with children with ASD, with supporting technology strategies defined as follows:

- *"Low" technology:* Visual support strategies that do not involve any type of electronic or battery-operated device—typically low-cost, easy-to-use equipment. Examples: dry-erase boards, clipboards, three-ring binders, manila file folders, photo albums, laminated PCS/photographs, and highlight tape.
- *"Mid" technology:* Battery-operated devices or simple electronic devices requiring limited advancements in technology. Examples: tape recorders, Drake Educational Associate's Language Master, overhead projectors, timers, calculators, and simple voice output devices.
- *"High" technology:* Complex technological support strategies—typically relatively high-cost equipment. Examples: video cameras, computers and adaptive hardware, and complex voice output devices.

Low-Tech Strategies

Increasing comprehension of tasks/activities/situations is essential in addressing skill areas such as organization, attending, self-help, following directions, following rules, and modifying behavior. As a result of understanding the world better, the child becomes more independent. The following low-tech visual support strategies can be used to assist the child in increasing comprehension skills, thus decreasing the occurrence of challenging behaviors.

Schedules

Consistent daily use of an individualized visual schedule will increase a child's organization skills and independent functioning throughout all aspects of life and will ease transition through adulthood. There are numerous ways to present visual schedules. Examples include object schedules, three-ring binder schedules, clipboard schedules, manila file folder schedules, and dry-erase board schedules.

Each child's individual needs should be considered in designing a personal visual schedule. It should be noted that visual schedules are as important for the child to use at school as at home. The information given to children through a visual mode is extremely critical in helping them to understand the day's events and their sequence.

A visual schedule will give the child the following information:

- What is currently happening
- What is coming up next (the sequence of events)
- When the child is "all done" with something
- Any changes that might occur

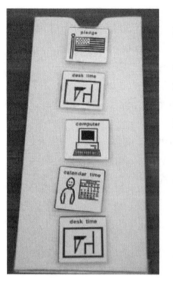

A visual schedule is a "first-then" strategy (that is, "first you do ___, then you do ___,) rather than an "if-then" approach (that is, "if you do ___, then you can do ___"). The "first" activity can be modified as needed to accommodate the child's changing ability to process incoming information. Once the first activity is done, then the child can move on to the next visually scheduled task/activity. It is important for children to indicate that they are "all done" with a scheduled activity. For example, they can cross out or check off the scheduled item or place the scheduled activity object/photo/ PCS in an "all done" envelope.

Various social interactions can be included in the child's daily schedule as well as building in a balance of "high-stress" (nonpreferred) and "low-stress" (preferred) activities. Each child's break time or quiet time can also be visually scheduled at various times throughout the day as needed.

> **Example.** The child may be required to show completed work to a teacher for social interaction and reinforcement or to say hello to the teacher and students when entering the classroom.

Mini-schedules/routines can also be incorporated as needed into the child's day.

> **Example.** A visual routine checklist titled "Before Kindergarten" was developed for a child who was having difficulty establishing a routine while waiting to go to kindergarten following lunch. As he did not readily comprehend what was expected of him during this time, challenging behaviors typically occurred. The routine was laminated and posted on the refrigerator with magnets glued to the back. The child would then check off each completed routine activity (e.g., eat lunch, wash face and hands, brush teeth, read two books, put on shoes and socks, put on coat and back pack, wait by the door for the bus).

Activity Schedules

Independently engaging in appropriate tasks/activities for a certain period of time is an important life skill for children with ASD. An activity schedule teaches this skill through a set of pictures (photo or PCS) or written words, which are used to cue the child visually to engage in a sequence of activities for independent recreation/leisure time.

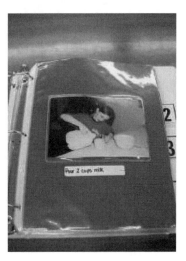

The number of activities and sequence of steps per activity need to be individualized for each child. For some children, activities will need to be broken down and depicted step-by-step for the child to complete the activity independently. For other children, a more general, single photo/PCS/written word can be used to cue the child to perform an entire task or activity. Any type of binder, photo album, etc., can be used as the child's activity schedule book, or simple written lists may suffice for the child who is able to read and comprehend. The activity schedule book should contain the various tasks/activities (and steps if needed) depicted in whatever visual representation system the child best comprehends (e.g., photos, line drawings, etc.). Upon completion, a social reinforcer can be built into the schedule as the last page in the book.

Example 1: On the first page of a photo album, a photograph of a puzzle is depicted. On the next page, a photo of a shape sorter is depicted. On the third page, there is a photo of the child being thrown up in the air by Daddy.

Example 2: A written list with the following items listed, to be checked/crossed off by the child: (1) Unload dishwasher, (2) Vacuum living room, (3) Fold towels, (4) Computer for 30 minutes.

Calendars (home/school)

Use of a weekly/monthly calendar at both home and school can provide children with important information regarding upcoming events/activities, rather than relying on auditory information. When children ask when a particular event (class field trips, bath night, McDonald's, etc.) will occur, they can easily be referred to the visual calendar.

Use of a visual calendar can also be helpful in assisting the child to understand when regularly scheduled events may not occur.

> **Example:** If the child has swim lessons every Friday after school, but this Friday, the pool is closed, draw an "international no" symbol—a circle with a slashed line through it—on the scheduled swim lesson.

In this example, acknowledgement is made that the child has a scheduled activity while communicating that it is not occurring on a particular day.

Calendars can also be used to give the child important information regarding school attendance, which is particularly helpful for days off from school during the typical school week. A monthly calendar is used that shows visually each day that the child will be at home or at school. Many parents put these monthly calendars on the refrigerator and reference them daily with their child by crossing off a completed day and noting where the child will be going (or staying) tomorrow.

In addition to schedules, comprehension skills can be increased by the following strategies.

"International No" Symbol

Use of the "international no" symbol (red circle with a line drawn through it) has proven very effective in visually communicating the very abstract concept of "no" for children with autism.

Use of the "international no" symbol can assist the child in visually comprehending the following:

"Stop—don't do what you are doing."

> **Example:** A behavior management card might show a picture communication symbol (PCS) of "no hitting" with an "international no" over it.

"That is not a choice right now."

> **Example:** If the child hands you a PCS of something that he or she wants and that is not an option at this time, use a red dry-erase marker to place an "international no" on the PCS and say, "No _____ not now."

"You are not permitted."

Example: Placement of a tagboard-size "international no" on doors has stopped children from running out the door.

"Nonexistence."

Example: Placement of the "international no" on a scheduled activity to acknowledge that, although the activity typically occurs at this time/day, it will not be occurring today—for whatever reason.

Directions

Low-tech strategies can be used in numerous ways to give the child visual information for following directions. Visual information greatly increases the child's comprehension of what is expected and is far more effective than auditory directions only. Visual directions help gain, maintain, and refocus a child's attention as well as ensuring that he or she gets complete instructions, thereby reducing the amount of support needed and increasing independent skills.

The following low-tech strategies can be used to give the child visually presented directions:

- Use of a dry-erase board or contact paper whiteboard covering part of a notebook or schedule system to write/draw various visual directions, which are also given orally

Example: Take out your journals. Write three sentences about your weekend. Raise your hand when you are finished.

- Sequential step directions for specific tasks/activities

Examples: Brushing teeth, making lunch, vacuuming, folding towels, setting the table, checking out books from the library, cooking, going about doing homework, getting ready for school in the morning

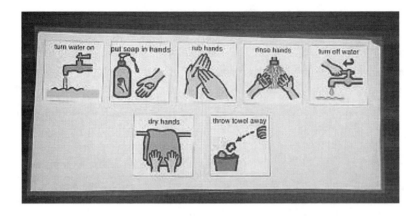

Example: School morning directions. Upon arrival at school, a child is given a "morning directions" card to assist him in completing a visual list of instructions before sitting at his desk and beginning the day. The card is laminated and has a dry-erase marker attached by a string. It is located near the child's coat hook. After hanging up his coat and backpack, he can take the card and begin the "morning directions," checking off each item upon completion (e.g., (1) Put reading book in tub; (2) Put attendance stick in box; (3) Put lunch ticket in hot/cold box; (4) Put "morning directions" card away; (5) Sit at desk.).

Example: Brushing teeth. PCS representing each sequential step in this task are placed on a Velcro strip positioned directly above the sink (in front of the child). As the child completes each step of the task, she pulls off the PCS representing the step completed and puts it in an "all done" envelope.

Example: Library. A small set of PCS represents the steps necessary to complete the library routine of choosing a book, checking the book out, sitting at a table and reading the book, and then walking back to class is created. This set of PCS is attached via a metal ring, which can easily be kept in the child's pocket or attached to a belt loop or binder for easy step-by-step reference when going to the library.

Example: Setting the table. Photographs of each sequential step for setting the table are placed in a small photo album accompanied by written directions. The last page should indicate something desirable for the child to do upon completion of this task, such as "computer for 30 minutes." The child is taught to turn each page after completing a step.

Forewarning

For children who need very explicit forewarning regarding when something is going to stop/end or be "all done," use of *go, almost done,* and *stop* cards have proven very effective in giving children this important information, thereby assisting them in making this sometimes difficult transition (to stop).

Strategy: Forewarning cards are particularly useful for activities that do not have clear-cut endings, such as some computer games, video games, drawing, etc.

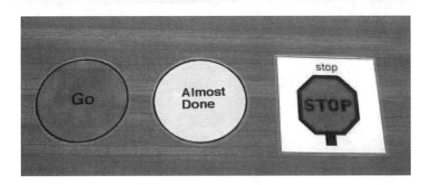

Each card is a large, colored circle with *go* as green, *almost done* as yellow, and *stop* as red, with the word written in large letters in the center of the colored circle. When the child starts an activity, the green *go* card is placed on his or her desk, computer table, etc., accompanied by a verbal message to go or start the task. When there are approximately 1–2 minutes left for the child to continue the activity, the *almost done* yellow circle is placed in front of the child, accompanied by a verbal message. When it is time to stop the activity, the red *stop* circle is placed in front of the child with the verbal message that it is time to stop.

Rules/Alternative Behaviors

Putting rules in a visual form allows the child to understand expectations, as well as what actions or alternatives are acceptable. This strategy results in more consistent behavior. In addition, visual representation of rules and alternative behaviors allows the child to improve his or her self-regulation and self-management skills without needing the support of an adult.

- *Class rules or individualized personal rules taped to desk:* These rules should be provided through a visual representation system that the child can understand (written words, line drawings, etc.). If the child is engaging in an inappropriate behavior, he or she can be directed to look at a specific rule (e.g., "Read rule number 3.")
- *"Good Choices That I Can Make" list:* This visual support strategy assists the child in understanding and making appropriate choices when he or she has "broken" rules or engaged in inappropriate behaviors. This list should be posted so that the child has easy visual access to it, and it should initially be referenced by an adult in the environment to teach the child the importance of this visual support strategy.

> **Example:** The child is making silly noises at the beginning of a math assignment, with math typically being a difficult subject for the child. An adult can direct the child to the appropriate rule that is visually represented on his desk, either by pointing to the rule or stating, "Look at rule number ___," which states, "Sit quietly and do my work." The adult should then reference the child's "Good Choices That I Can Make" list. The adult may initially need to point out which choice the child should make in this circumstance.

This strategy will greatly assist the child in developing behavioral self-management skills. The following "Good Choices That I Can Make" list is an example:

1. I can raise my hand to ask questions or get help.
2. I can ask more questions if I still don't understand.
3. If I don't understand what someone is saying or doing, I can ask them.
4. I know that my own words and actions can make people feel differently than I do.
5. I can use *I* messages to tell people how I feel. ("I feel bad when you tell me recess will be inside.")
6. I can write down the problem and then think of appropriate things that I could do.
7. I could use relaxation strategies. "Take a deep breath, count to ten, breathe out slowly."
8. I could ask for time-out (break) all by myself.

9. I can make good choices.

- *Individual rule/behavior cards:* These visual representation cards can be kept on a metal ring and used when needed either singly or in succession. The "international no" should be drawn in red on top of the PCS or photo when appropriate to indicate clearly that a specific behavior should not occur. Behavior management cards can also be color coded. This gives the child additional visual information to understand better desired and undesired behaviors. The following colors are used:

    o *Red:* Behaviors you *don't* want the child to do (e.g., "no throwing").

    o *Yellow:* Behaviors you request the child to demonstrate (e.g., "Shhh, quiet," "Quiet hands").

    o *Green:* Appropriate alternative choices (e.g., "Give a hug," "Take a walk.").

> **Example:** Use a picture communication symbol (PCS) laminated on large index cards to communicate the following:
> "Look at Mrs. Jones"—PCS of eyes
> "Sit on chair"—PCS of a child sitting in a chair
> "Shh, be quiet"—PCS of a face with its finger to lips indicating "Shh"
> "Don't hit"—"international no" drawn on top of PCS of a child hitting another child

Transition Rule Cards

These cards can be used to help the children understand (visually) where they are going and what is expected of them in this environment.

> **Example: Going to McDonald's.** A photograph of McDonald's is laminated to an index card. On the back of the card, specific rules for going to McDonald's are visually represented.

- *If something is bothering me I can . . . :* This strategy visually helps the child choose appropriate alternative behaviors when anxious or stressed. This card can be taped to the child's desk with the above heading and the following examples, or it can be placed in a small photo album, which may also contain other visual support strategies:
  o Raise my hand for help
  o Close my eyes and count to ten
  o Take five big breaths
  o Ask for a break

Expressive Communication Skills

Low-tech strategies designed to focus on a child's expressive communication skills include the following:

- *Picture point communication board system:* To communicate, the child points to various visual representations (e.g., photos, PCS, objects, etc.) located on a "communication board." Numerous communication boards can be created that are child-, task-, or environment-specific.

> **Examples:** A place mat communication board can be used during snacks and meals with PCS around the edge of the place mat. A communication board can be created for the play area.

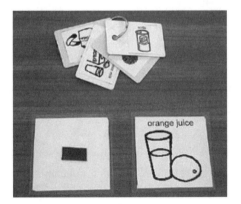

- *Picture Exchange Communication System (PECS):* The child approaches and gives a picture of a desired item (photo, PCS, object, etc.) to a communicative partner in exchange for that item. The use of this type of communication system provides the child with a way to communicate and, most importantly, teaches the child to initiate a functional communicative exchange spontaneously.

  Numerous adaptations can be made when using a PECS program to meet the individual needs of a child. For example, placing the visual representation system on frozen juice can lids or other hard discs or squares (countertop samples) allows the visual representation system to become more prominent to children by giving them more tactile input (weight and hardness). They may tend to crumple up lightweight paper items (pictures on plain paper), possibly to meet a sensory need.

- *Break cards:* These help children communicate that they need some downtime or a break. Break cards should be easily accessible to the child and should be located in a consistent spot in the classroom, such as on the child's communication board or book, on the child's desk, etc. The purpose of the break card is for children to communicate that they need a break by using an appropriate communicative mode (visual representation system) rather than becoming increasingly anxious and frustrated, which may result in the occurrence of challenging behaviors.

- *Choice cards:* Choice cards (again using any type of visual representation system) allow the child to exercise a degree of independence by choosing from a predetermined set of possibilities. For example, a "work time" choice card could be presented to the child with several choices of activities for the child to choose from. When presented in this manner, children are less likely to act out, because they are allowed to choose what they want to do.

- *"All done" cards:* Many nonverbal children exhibit challenging behaviors to indicate that they are all done with something, as they typically have no other way to communicate this concept. Therefore, teaching a more appropriate way to indicate "all done" through a visual representation system will lessen both the child's and adult's stress and frustration. "All done" cards can be taped to the child's work area and taught to the child by stopping an activity prior to child's reaching her attention/frustration level, then pointing to the "all done" card. The child's hand can be physically prompted to point to the "all done" card if needed. "All done" cards can also be placed on the child's communication board or book for her to use.

- *Topic ring/topic wallet:* These are designed for children who are verbal yet have difficulty initiating a topic with others or have difficulty initiating various topics with others, particularly when these topics are not related to their high-interest areas. The topic wallet/ring can have various topics visually illustrated (e.g., written words, PCS) to prompt the child to initiate a topic.

> **Example:** The following topics are illustrated individually on small 3" × 3" laminated cards using both PCS and written words. They are either attached by a metal ring in the corner (for the child to hook on a belt loop) or placed in a small "communication wallet" to be kept in his pocket. The topics could include "What did you do over the weekend?" "What is your favorite movie?" "Do you have any pets?" and "What books do you like to read?"

- *Relating past events:* Many children with ASD, both verbal and nonverbal, have significant difficulty relating past events. Using a visual representation system that the child readily understands can help to bridge this gap, at least between home and school. General templates that can be easily circled or filled out each day and sent to the respective location (home or school) aid the child in relating past information through this visual representation system.

Social Skills

Children with ASD need to be directly taught various social skills in one-to-one and/or small-group settings. Numerous low-tech strategies can be used for this purpose. Social skills training must also consider the child's possible difficulties in generalizing this information to different social situations. Generalization may be supported through the following visual strategies:

- *Social stories:* Social stories, developed by Carol Gray, provide children with visual information/strategies that will improve their understanding of various social situations and teach them specific behaviors to use when interacting with others. Social stories are written in first person and are individually written for each child for various difficult social situations (for example, staying in an assigned seat on the bus). The social story should be visually represented in a mode that the child can most readily understand (e.g., written words, line drawings and written words, or photos and written words).

  The repetitious reading of the Social Story, when the child is calm, is what leads to the success of this strategy. Two three-ring binders of identical social stories, kept in page protectors, could be made, one for home and one for school, so the child can read them at leisure. This strategy has proven to be very successful for many students in learning to recognize, interpret, and interact appropriately in different social situations.

  A software program from Slater Software Company, which converts text to a graphic symbol, is called Picture It. This software program is ideal for adding line drawing graphics above written words to increase the child's understanding of social stories.
- *Social scripts:* Social scripts are similar to social stories; however, an actual script is developed for a specific child in a specific social situation.

> **Example:** A child has difficulty asking peers if he can join in their "ball-tag" game at recess. He typically runs into the middle of the game, takes the ball, and then runs away. The script would read: Joey—"Hi guys. Can I play ball-tag with you?" Guys—"Sure you can, Joey, but you will have to wait over there until it's your turn to throw the ball." Joey—"OK, I'll wait until you tell me it's my turn."

  Use of social scripts also helps in role-playing various social situations with peers, puppets, etc. Social scripts can also be used to visually, thus clearly, indicate what went wrong in a social situation.
- *Comic strip conversations:* Simple drawings can be used to clarify visually the elements of social interactions and emotional relations. Comic strip conversations are used to work through a problem situation visually and identify solutions.

- *Turn-taking cards:* Turn-taking cards are used to represent visually whose turn it is. Turn-taking cards with a visual representation mode (PCS, object, written word, etc.) is very effective in teaching this social skills concept.
- *"Wait" cards:* Wait cards visually represent the abstract concept of "waiting" through the use of a large, orange oval card printed with the word *wait*. These cards can be used in any situation.

Examples: Place the wait card on the computer monitor while waiting for the computer or a program to boot up. Have the child hold the wait card while waiting in line.

- *"Help" cards:* Help cards are used to teach children the abstract concept of raising their hands to indicate that they need help. Initially, it is necessary to provide a concrete reason for children to raise their hands by using the "help" card. A visual representation of "I need help" (PCS, photograph, or written word taped to a Popsicle stick or object) is given to children to raise up in the air to indicate that they need help. The item that they raise in the air can gradually be eliminated, until the children are readily raising only their hands to seek assistance.
- *"Waiting hands" card:* An outline of a person's open hands on colored paper is used as a guideline as to where the children should place their hands while waiting (for their turn, for a chance to perform an action, etc.).
- *Social "rule" cards:* These cards are taped to the child's desk in the classroom. They say things like "I will raise my hand and wait for the teacher to call on me." Social rule cards can be

made for environments other than just the classroom. One rule card per environment can be written on an index card, laminated, and then given to the child to carry as a visual reminder of the social rules for that particular situation.

> **Example:** Library social rules card: "I will sit at a table with at least one other student," "I will discuss my book with one other student," "I will discuss another student's book."

Attending Skills

The visual symbols for *go, almost done,* and *stop* can also be used to increase a child's attending skills. Data will need to be obtained first to get a general idea of how long a child attends to a particular task.

> **Example:** The child attends to a particular task for approximately 45 seconds and then throws all of his materials to indicate that he is "all done." To teach the significance of the *go , almost done,* and *stop* cards, the *go* card is given at the start of the activity, the *almost done* card is given after approximately 30 seconds (as we already know the child will throw the materials after 45 seconds), and the *stop* card is given at approximately 40 seconds, with the activity immediately ceasing. It is critical to use the cards initially to stop the activity *prior* to the child's throwing the materials so that the child realizes the significance of the cards in relaying the messages of being "almost done" and "stopping." Gradually, the length of time before giving the child the *almost done* card and the *stop* card is increased, thus increasing the child's attending skills. It is important to note that the *almost done* card is always given to the child within a short time of giving him the *stop* card. Consistency is important in using these cards to increase the child's attention.

Academics

- *File folder activities:* The use of file folder activities can assist the child to focus independently on numerous academic tasks. Long strips of Velcro are placed on the inside pages of a laminated file folder. Matching tasks focusing on colors, shapes, alphabet letters, common nouns, familiar people, categories, relationships (e.g., between shoes and socks), etc. can be developed for the child, as well as tasks focusing on reading comprehension skills, math skills, generalization skills, etc.
- *Highlighter tape:* Many children with ASD possess relative strengths in their reading recognition skills (decoding) but

experience significant difficulty understanding what they have read (comprehension). Highlighter tape is a removable transparent tape that can be used to highlight text in an economical, nondestructive way. For example, the tape can be to highlight key words pertaining to a reading comprehension question. Different colors of highlight tape can be used to encode different significant concepts (e.g., blue highlight tape to mark dates, yellow highlight tape to mark people, etc.).

Mid-Tech Strategies

Listed below are descriptions of several mid-tech devices that children with ASD can use to enhance specific skill areas. Most of these devices are very appealing to these children and provide them with motivation to participate and focus on various skills and classroom activities successfully. These devices are called voice output communication aids (VOCAs). Any type of visual representation system can be placed on simple voice output devices for children to access by a simple push of a "button." Most of these devices are battery operated and are easy to operate for recording messages. It is important to note that these devices were created for use as an augmentative means to communicate expressively. However, for many children with ASD, they work well in numerous ways to focus attention on various skill areas, as well as increase classroom participation, focus, and communication. The following list identifies a number of such mid-tech VOCA devices:

- *Big Mack:* A single switch/button device available from AbleNet that allows for 20 seconds of recording time. Approximate cost is $89.
- *Talk Pad:* A four-message/button battery-operated device available that allows for 15 seconds of recording time per button. Available from Frame Technologies for approximately $99.

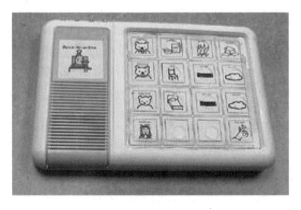

- *Voice in the Box:* Multimessage battery-operated communication devices available in 16, 24, or 40 messages/buttons from Frame Technologies for approximately $195.
- *Cheap Talk 4:* A four-message/button device that allows for five seconds of recording time per button. Available from Enabling Devices for approximately $69.
- *Step-by-Step:* A battery-operated device that allows for prerecording a series of unlimited sequenced messages up to a total of 75 seconds of recording time. Available from AbleNet for $129.

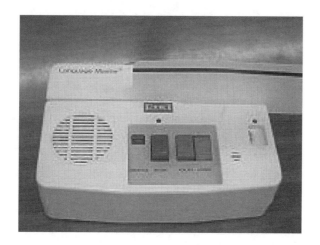

- *Language Master:* The Language Master has been used for more than 20 years. It is an electronic device about the size of an old tape recorder. The cards, which are approximately 3" × 8" with a recordable strip across the bottom, are played "through" the Language Master. A short verbal message can be recorded on each card. The cards are also big enough to include corresponding visual cues (e.g., words, PCS, photos) of the recorded message. Available from Drake Educational for $295.
- *Tape recorder:* Any easily operated tape recorder can be effective in addressing various skill areas in children with ASD.

VOCAs can be used to develop the following groups of skills for children with ASD: language comprehension skills, expressive communication skills, social skills, attending skills, organization skills, and academic skills. The following is a discussion of these skill areas and the possible use of specific VOCAs to help children with ASD function more independently.

Language Comprehension Skills

- *Talk Pad:* This device can be programmed according to simple four-step directions. The child is motivated to hit the buttons and thus complete the sequence of steps.

> **Example:** A child with ASD experiences great difficulty following the three-step sequence to complete his "job," which is to prepare for snack time. The child requires continual verbal and physical prompting from an adult to attend to the task—as the child typically runs around the room—and then to complete each step of the task. The three steps of the task are recorded on the Talk Pad, with the fourth message telling the child to "sit in chair." Visual cues, corresponding with each verbal message, are placed on top of each "button" on the Talk Pad with Velcro. The child is extremely motivated to "push the buttons" on this device and, following the initial teaching, is now able to do his "job" independently for snack time.

- *Language Master:* The teacher may record multistep directions on the cards, one step per card. If students cannot remember the auditory directions that were given, they can run the cards through the Language Master to hear some or all of the directions.

Expressive Communication Skills

- *Voice Output Communication Aid (VOCA):* Children can express themselves with the assistance of any visual representation mode or via visual cues placed on a VOCA. Many children with ASD are motivated to communicate by use of these devices, particularly by the auditory feedback immediately given as they use the device. VOCAs have proven effective in teaching children the cause-and-effect of language through activities that are stimulating.

> **Example:** A child with ASD could use the Big Mack to request highly desired sensory activities, such as "chase me," "tickle me," "hug me," and "listen to music."

VOCAs are not always effective for all children with ASD. Some children find the VOCAs overly motivating and stimulating, so they do not become effective communication devices. The child may repeatedly push the button(s) on the device for the self-motivation from the auditory feedback rather than for the cause-and-effect of the communicative message. In this case, the VOCAs can still be used with the child, since they are clearly motivating, but in a different manner. For example, they may be used to focus attention on various skill areas, as well as increase classroom participation. In this case, the child's communication needs may be more effectively addressed through the use of low-tech expressive communication strategies.

A research study evaluating the use of VOCAs by children with ASD revealed the following:

  o Young children with ASD can learn to use VOCAs effectively to communicate various language functions (e.g., request, answer yes/no questions, make social comments).

  o VOCA use can be generalized across settings.

  o Use of VOCAs increases the child's use of gestures, words, and vocalizations.

  o Communication partner interactions increased when VOCAs were used.

- *Audiotaping:* Audiotaping can be used to focus on communication skills and draw the child's attention to an inappropriate communicative behavior. (e.g., interrupting, perseverative speech, incessant question asking, topic maintenance, etc.), as well as to develop self-awareness and self-regulation of appropriate communicative interactions.

- *Language Master:* For a child who is able to imitate, the Language Master could be used as a model for imitation, as well as to provide an opportunity to engage in social interactions.

Example: At the end of a child's activity schedule book is a Language Master card with a picture of bubbles glued on and the written words, "I want bubbles." The child places the card in the Language Master and then takes the card and gives it to someone while repeating the utterance. In return for the card, the child receives a bubble-blowing toy.

Social Skills

- *Big Mack:* This piece of equipment is a great motivational device to focus on turn-taking activities. Countless turn-taking activities can be created and incorporated into every aspect of the school day.

> **Example:** During circle time, children can take turns pushing the Big Mack button to respond to prerecorded calendar routines (What day is it? What month is it?), songs (using repetitive lines works great for this activity: "Old McDonald had a farm..."), and books ("Turn the page" during large-group reading). "My turn" can be used as a visual/physical marker when focusing on specific turn-taking tasks, and so forth.

- *Audiotaping:* Any type of social interaction, both appropriate and inappropriate, can be taped and then replayed as a teaching method to assist the child in identifying what is an appropriate, and what is inappropriate, social communicative behavior. Social communicative behaviors include interrupting, asking for assistance, drawing attention, initiating varied topics, and maintaining topics initiated by others. Audiotaping may also be used to focus on various nonverbal social communication skills, such as maintaining an appropriate vocal volume or emotional tone of voice.

Attending Skills (Motivation)

- *Voice in the Box:* This device can help children to focus their attention during large-group listening activities. These activities tend to be very difficult for children with ASD. Again, countless activities can be created and incorporated into any large-group listening time.

> **Example:** When the teacher is reading a book aloud to the class, numerous lines from a book can be visually represented with a corresponding recorded message on the buttons. The child can "assist" in "reading" the story by pushing the appropriate buttons for the story. Repetitive line books such as *Brown Bear* work great. The child can push the button for "Brown Bear, Brown Bear what do you see?" Another example would be the line "but he was still hungry" from *The Very Hungry Caterpillar.* Circle time activities can be programmed in a similar manner.

- *Big Mack:* To increase attention during large-group listening/reading activities, record a repetitive line from a story and place a corresponding visual representation system on top of the Big Mack.

> **Example:** A picture of the Big Bad Wolf was placed on the Big Mack switch that played the repetitive line "I'll huff and I'll puff and I'll blow your house down."

- *VOCAs as Reinforcement:* Many students with ASD find the VOCAs to be very reinforcing. If allowed to interact with the VOCA upon completion of less-desirable tasks, they find the necessary motivation to attend to and complete those tasks.

Organization Skills (Story Sequencing and Time Management)

- *Talk Pad:* The physical layout of the "buttons" on this device works well for focusing on sequence stories, because the four buttons are positioned from left-to-right. The Cheap Talk 4 works somewhat less well, because the buttons are located two above and two below.

  Each step of a sequence story can be prerecorded on each of the four buttons in sequential order. The four corresponding sequence story pictures are placed in front of the child not in order. As the child presses the first button in the left-to-right sequence of buttons, he or she hears the auditory message for the first sequence picture. The student can then select the picture corresponding to that message as the first picture in the sequence story and place it on top of the first button using Velcro. This continues with each of the subsequent buttons and pictures. Printed sentences can also be used in place of pictures for the sequence story.

- *Language Master:* The Language Master provides a motivating and novel approach to focus on sequence stories, typically a difficult activity for a child with ASD. The child listens to the sentence on the card describing a picture, which is part of a sequence story. The child can then put the appropriate picture in sequential order for the story, according to the message given on the Language Master.

Academics

- *Talk Pad:* This device can be used as a motivating way to focus the child's attention on phonics. Each button can be prerecorded with a sound from a three- to four-sound word (e.g., d–o–g). The child then chooses the corresponding letter card to match with the recorded sound

Example: The first button of the Talk Pad is recorded with the sound /d/. The child chooses from a selection of the three letters that comprise *dog*, as well as the entire written word, and places the matching letter on the first button (using Velcro). The child progresses through each button in the same manner. The final button makes the machine say, "Dog," and the child matches the whole written word, *dog*, to this final button.

- *Voice in the Box:* This motivating device can be used in numerous ways to focus on various academic skills.

> **Example:** Varied levels of reading comprehension skills can be addressed, from matching simple single pictures to corresponding written words to answering questions regarding various written information. For example, animal pictures can be Velcroed to a top-to-bottom button column on the Voice in the Box, with corresponding words recorded under each button. When the child presses one of the pictures, such as a picture of a dog, the recorded button message says, "Dog, find the word *dog.*" The child must then choose which written word matches the picture and its auditory message and place that written word (using Velcro) on the blank button next to the picture of the dog. When the child places the written word *dog*, on the blank button, the button responds with a prerecorded message of "d–o–g, dog."

High-Tech Strategies

Two high-tech strategies have proven very effective in focusing on various skill areas for children with ASD: videotaping and computers.

Videotaping

Children with ASD are often highly interested, motivated, and thus attentive to videos. Many children enjoy repetitive viewing of videos due to the predictability of the information given; that is, they enjoy knowing what's coming up next. Thus videotaping can serve as an excellent tool with which to teach numerous skills to children with ASD. These skills may include the following:

- *Language comprehension skills:* Receptive vocabulary skills can be taught through videotaping (names of common everyday objects, toys, names of familiar people, animals). Directions to complete various routines can also be taught by the same videotaping strategy (e.g., making the bed, setting the table, getting dressed, going to the library).
- *Social skills:* Numerous social situations can be videotaped and replayed to teach identification of appropriate and inappropriate social behaviors. Videotaped segments can be made of any social area in which the child might be experiencing difficulties (e.g., asking for assistance, initiating varied topics, maintaining topics initiated by others, repetitive/perseverative speech or question asking, interrupting others).

  Nonverbal features of social communication can also be taught effectively through videotaping (e.g., tone of voice, facial expressions, body postures/language, gestures, personal space, vocal volume).

  In addition, videotaping can be used to demonstrate how to engage and/or interact appropriately in various social contexts, such as recess, lunch, music class, McDonald's, church, etc.
- *Expressive language skills:* Expressive vocabulary skills (e.g., names of items, people, places) can be taught in much the same way as receptive vocabulary skills. The teaching of categorization skills and concepts as well as pragmatic language skills (social interaction skills) can be enhanced through the use of videotaping.
- *Self-help skills:* Self-help skills, such as getting dressed, brushing teeth, washing hands, even practicing good hygiene, can be demonstrated through the use of videotaping.
- *Emotions:* Facial expressions showing various emotional states can be videotaped and shown to demonstrate various feelings.
- *Academics:* Writing skills, such as drawing shapes, writing alphabet letters, writing words (names of familiar nouns), and story generation, can also be demonstrated and taught through videotaping.

Computers

Research on the use of computers with students with ASD revealed the following:

- Increase in focused attention
- Increase in overall attention span
- Increase in in-seat behavior
- Increase in fine motor skills
- Increase in generalization of skills (from computer to related noncomputer activities)
- Decrease in agitation
- Decrease in self-stimulatory behaviors
- Decrease in perseverative responses

Many students with ASD are highly interested and motivated by computers. Therefore, computers should be infused into the child's daily curriculum, not used solely for reward or recreational purposes. Computer-assisted learning can focus on numerous academic areas as well as provide an appropriate independent leisure time activity for people with ASD.

- *Adaptive hardware:* To access the computer, some children with ASD might require that the standard computer be adapted with certain devices. Listed below are a variety of devices that can assist a child in accessing the computer:
  - *Touch window:* The purpose of the touch window is to allow the child to navigate and interact with the computer by touching the screen rather than operating the mouse. A touch window/screen can be easily mounted on the computer monitor and the user simply touches the screen to replace mouse actions. The use of a touch screen can assist a student who experiences difficulty understanding the abstract relationship between the mouse movement and the resulting actions on the screen. With a touch screen, the concrete relationship between what the child sees and touches and what happens is established. The Touch Window is available for Macintosh or Windows platforms from Edmark for approximately $335.
  - *Intellikeys:* This is a commonly used alternative keyboard that easily connects to a computer and is available for Macintosh or Windows platforms. To operate the computer, the child simply pushes various locations on an overlay that is placed

in the Intellikeys. Standard overlays for the alphabet, numbers, mouse direction, and a "single switch hit" are included with the Intellikeys. However, various overlays can also be created to go with numerous software programs through the purchase and use of additional Intellitools software programs. In addition to acting as an alternative keyboard, the Intellikeys has four switch jacks located on the side of the keyboard, so that a single switch or multiple switches can be connected to the computer through the Intellikeys for children to access via a single switch hit. This technology allows children with limited fine motor control to access the computer. The Intellikeys is available from Intellitools for approximately $350.

o *Big Keys and Big Keys Plus:* This alternative alphabet keyboard has been designed specifically for young children. The keys are large (one inch square), with the various alphabet letters color coded to help children more readily find specific keys (e.g., vowels in one color, consonants in a different color). The keyboard is also arranged in ABC order for easy access for younger children. This keyboard is available from Greystone Digital for approximately $150.

o *Trackballs:* Trackballs come in various sizes and shapes and allow children to move the mouse around the screen by rolling a stationary ball around with either their fingertips or hands. Some children with ASD can master the mouse operations with a trackball and eventually transfer to use of a standard mouse. Trackballs can be purchased from many retailers for approximately $40–$100.

o *Software:* Numerous software programs are available that focus on a variety of skill areas: language skills, attending skills, problem-solving skills, fine motor skills, academic skills, and leisure time activities.

• *Accessory Equipment*

o *Digital camera:* A digital camera can be very beneficial in making two-dimensional visual representation systems for children who have a strong preference for visually presented information.

o *Scanner:* A scanner can be used to scan in numerous materials, such as pages from books, assignment sheets, CD covers, video covers, etc. Once the item is scanned, it can be shown as text or as a graphic on the computer, allowing the child to access it through the keyboard.

Conclusion

It is interesting to note that the majority of strategies listed in this chapter fall under the category of "low" technology and should therefore be easily accessible to many at a relatively low cost. It is important to consider that all of these suggestions, from low-tech to high-tech, should always be individualized to meet the unique needs of any child with ASD. Most importantly, use of these varied modes of technology will greatly increase the child's independent functioning skills by decreasing the amount of direct support needed from another person.

15

Behavior and Discipline Issues for Students With ASD

M ost students with ASD want to behave appropriately and follow the rules but have a great deal of trouble applying their rote memory of rules to real situations, especially when they are anxious, impulsive, or confused. Students with ASD have trouble understanding how to apply school and social rules, even though some students with verbal language and good memory may be able to recite the very rules they seem to break. In some cases, these students may correct others who break the rules—at least the rules that are very specific and concrete. Because of this variability in understanding rules and actual performance of appropriate behaviors, educators, family, and peers often are unsure about how to apply discipline to students with ASD. Typical questions related to behavior and discipline for students with ASD include the following:

- How do you develop appropriate behaviors for students with ASD?
- What do we do when a student with ASD engages in inappropriate behaviors?

- Are the standards of discipline applied to students who are not disabled also applied to a student with ASD?

Developing Appropriate Behaviors for Students With ASD

It is the responsibility of the Individualized Education Program (IEP) committee to determine the specific goals, objectives, and specially designed instruction related to behavior that will enable the student with ASD to be successful in learning environments. The decisions concerning behavior development will be reflected on the student's IEP. The IEP committee and the multidisciplinary team determine which strategies will support the development of appropriate behaviors based upon the goals. Understanding ASD is imperative to providing the supports necessary for a student to be successful at home, school, and work and in the community. Each student with ASD will have unique needs in relationship to behavior and discipline. However, there are likely to be similarities in the types of problems. One way to get started developing or improving student behavior is to plan ahead for every student to understand behaviors, expectations, and rules. Some students will catch on to the expectations and rules, while others will need time and practice to get their behavior skills aligned with expectations and rules. The best place to begin in developing appropriate behaviors is with a plan.

Behavior Plan Key Idea: Use a Proactive Approach

Using a proactive approach means setting the stage for all students to be successful. It requires building an environment where the students learn the right behaviors before they have a chance to get them wrong. The proactive approach means *teaching* the students the precise behaviors expected for each rule. For example:

> *Every year, Ms. Wolf starts the first day of school teaching the students certain rules. One rule she teaches is: sit in your seat. She demonstrates for the students what she means by "in your seat." She explains that "sit" in your seat has three parts: (1) feet flat on the ground, (2) back against the back of the chair, and (3) hands on top of the desk. She lets each student practice the*

three steps and reinforces them for every step. Ms. Wolf also provides a picture sequence of the three steps for each student. Some students tape the pictures to their desks to remind them of the three steps. Because she puts the behavior into three steps, she can reinforce a student if at least one of the three behaviors is happening and then guide that student to completion of all three steps.

To create a proactive approach to behavior development, consider these steps.

1. Determine the Specific Rules That Must Be in Place for Learning to Occur

Classroom teachers need to identify what basic rules absolutely must be part of expectations for learning to occur. For example: One teacher lists five specific expectations or rules that are always in place in the classroom:

1. Keep your hands, feet, and materials within your personal space.

2. One person talks at a time.

3. Use a quiet, or three-inch, voice when talking with partners.

4. Listen to the teacher (or whoever is speaking to the class).

5. Use the polite words (e.g., please, thank you, may I).

To help Bruce understand those rules, the classroom teacher provides pictures of each rule for the class and particularly for Bruce. In addition, the teacher teaches each rule and helps the students practice each rule.

Family members need to identify what basic rules must be in effect at home. For example, Bruce's family has three general rules:

1. Get along with others.

2. Do your job without being asked.

3. Clean your room.

While these rules might be clear to the other children in the family, Bruce will likely need a more functional definition of what the rules mean for him. The family has further defined, in more specific terms, what these rules mean for Bruce. For example, Bruce learned that Rule 1 means no hitting or taking toys, Rule 2 means taking out the trash bag after dinner each night, and Rule 3 means putting every toy into his blue toy box before bed.

2. Understand the Student in Relationship to That Student's Unique Qualities (Strengths and Weaknesses)

Once specific behaviors or expectations have been determined, it is important to analyze the student's strengths and potential problems that may interfere with his or her ability to meet the expectation. Knowing potential problem areas gives guidance toward how expectations should be taught. Once the specific expectations and the capabilities of the student are known, decisions can be made concerning what must be taught and how it should be taught.

Risk Factors

Students with ASD face certain risk factors, which, if unaddressed, can pose problems related to behavior and discipline. The first risk factor to assess is personal challenges. For students with ASD, appropriate behavior may be impeded by the following problems:

- Understanding social interaction patterns; perspective, motives, and thinking of others; inappropriate or misinterpreted behaviors
- Learning sequentially
- Understanding language, especially abstract language, long sentences, and questions
- Expressing basic wants, needs, and feelings (especially when put on the spot)
- Understanding the passage of time or thinking through future events without support and rehearsal
- Processing and integrating problems that may make multisensory environments difficult and stressful
- Taking longer than their peers to process, organize, and retrieve information
- Developing inconsistently within and across domain and skill areas
- Applying learning across settings and people
- Using motor planning or having other motor problems
- Paying attention; not shifting attention or engaging attention; disengaging attention easily

- Becoming anxious and upset when not understanding a situation or feeling unsuccessful
- Taking a rule stated in the negative and knowing what to do

Certain environmental challenges, if not addressed, can pose problems for students with ASD. These challenges include the following:

- People who misunderstand the student's challenges
- Inconsistency (e.g., different rules and approaches from day to day, place to place, person to person; abstract, nonspecified rules that are not applied across teachers and settings)
- Confusing, disorganized environments (e.g., too much movement, clutter, loud music, noise, chaos)
- Punitive approaches to behavior management (e.g., abstract connections between negative punishment and student behavior; consequences that heighten the inappropriate or other behavior)
- Abstract guidelines for behavior
- Negative rules (e.g., rules that state what not to do instead of what the student should do, such as "Do not get out of your seat.")

Protective Factors

Once the personal and environmental challenges that may interfere with a student's appropriate behavior have been identified, it is important to look at the protective factors (personal resources and environmental resources) that enable developing and sustaining positive behaviors.

Personal resources are one key to developing positive behaviors in students with ASD. Educators, family, and peers must be aware of what the student knows, likes, and can do. These resources set the foundation for appropriate behaviors. A few simple steps for identifying and building personal resources follow:

- Identify, develop, and expand the student's strengths, interests, and preferences.
- Start with the skills the student has and gradually build his or her behavior repertoire.
- Take time to help the student adjust to new situations and activities.
- Encourage students to engage in activities that peers are doing and that the family does with individualized expectations and supports.

Not only is it important to understand and build upon a student's personal resources, it is equally important to develop the environmental resources that will support the student in developing and using positive behaviors.

Environmental resources are the other key to developing positive behaviors for students with ASD. Once potential problems and potential strengths of the student are determined, attention can turn to the environment. At this point it is important to determine what can be changed within the environment to support student learning. Questions to ask include these:

- What in this environment is making this behavior or rule so difficult to follow?
- Are there any unexpected triggers (e.g., noise, smells) within the environment?
- Does the environment consistently require this behavior, or is there inconsistency in expectations?
- What supports need to be in place to create success (e.g., time, pace, size, participation, difficulty, materials)?
- What are the least-intrusive supports (easiest to implement) that will produce success (e.g., put pictures of the behavior on the student's desk and provide a menu of reinforcers for appropriate behaviors)?
- What more-intrusive supports may be needed to produce success (e.g., new and complex behavior management system)?

3. Develop a Plan to Teach Positive Behavior

It is important when preparing to teach a new expectation that the specific behavior is clear, concise, and stated in a positive way. In addition to stating the behavior or expectation clearly, it is important to develop the plan to teach the behavior in a variety of ways so the student can learn the behavior. For example, some students will learn best by watching another student or teacher model the behavior, others may learn best by practicing the behavior, and still others might learn best when the expectation is written or drawn with specific steps. If a behavior or expectation has abstract implications, the plan must include teaching the behavior starting in concrete terms and moving to abstract terms. Many students will not immediately understand abstract concepts and may need multiple practice sessions before the behavior expectation is understood. Any plan to teach a new or desired behavior should include these steps:

1. Identify the appropriate behavior.

2. Teach the behavior using methods that match the student's learning style and needs.

3. Teach the cues for the behavior (e.g., when the teacher raises his or her hand with the palm out, it means to be silent/stop talking).

4. Practice the behavior (e.g., let students demonstrate for or critique each other). Allow time to get used to a situation through repeated trials.

5. Reinforce the behavior (e.g., provide verbal praise, award points).

6. Practice and reinforce the behavior across multiple settings

4. Create a Consistent, Predictable, Organized Environment

Once the behaviors have been taught, practiced, and reinforced across multiple settings, it is essential that the learning environment keep the expectations of behavior consistent. When a learning environment is organized and predictable, students will be better able to follow specific rules and understand the expectations within that environment. Consistency and predictability are essential for students with ASD to learn and succeed in any environment.

5. Collect Ongoing Data Related to Behaviors

Data collection is important for two reasons

1. When specific behavior goals are written on an IEP, the implementers are responsible for collecting data about when and how often behaviors are occurring. Keeping specific data allows the multidisciplinary team to evaluate the student's progress objectively. Information on the student's progress allows the team to make decisions for continuing or changing the goals of the student's IEP.

2. Data collection provides a view of the actual behaviors and progress the student makes on a daily and weekly basis. The data can provide the multidisciplinary team the information necessary to provide appropriate supports for the student to be successful in daily learning.

What to Do When a Student With ASD Engages in Inappropriate Behavior

The course of action to take when any student engages in inappropriate behavior depends upon the severity of the behavior. If the behavior threatens the physical well-being of the student, other students, or adults (e.g., stabbing with scissors), it may be necessary to intervene immediately to stop or prevent injury. If the behavior is not threatening (e.g., getting out of seat, taking others' toys), there are several options.

When a student with ASD engages in an inappropriate behavior, it is important to understand the purpose of the behavior. Refrain from getting into power struggles with the student. The student with ASD often seems to be intractable when engaged in unacceptable behaviors. Personal and environmental challenges can have a big impact on student behavior. The behavior should be analyzed to determine possible personal and environmental challenges contributing to the behavior.

Determine the Appropriate Behavior

Ask questions such as the following:

- What behaviors are absolutely essential for the student's safety and for the safety of others (e.g., stay within boundaries, walk beside someone, hold someone's hand, keep inedibles out of the mouth)?
- What behaviors are essential to the well-being of others (e.g., use words or gestures rather than yelling, hitting, or kicking)?
- What behaviors are needed to be successful with peers (e.g., attend to things that other students attend to, be aware of others, be near others, sit with others, play with others, communicate with others)?
- What behaviors are needed to take part in school activities (e.g., ride a bus, walk in a line, organize belongings, work quietly at times, take turns, ask for help, tolerate noises, make changes)?
- What behaviors will help the student keep learning (e.g., attend to certain activities and things, be toilet trained, use instruments, work independently, finish work)?
- What behaviors will build self-esteem in the student (e.g., paint a picture, climb and go down a slide, help, pass out the snacks, learn something that is exciting, be in a play, get all the spelling words right)?

Analyze the Purpose of Inappropriate Behavior

Try to figure out what the behavior means from the student's point of view. This is not easy, because individuals with ASD learn and view the world differently. Ask questions related to the risk factors and protective factors of the student. Here are just a few questions to ask:

- Is the student missing information that would enable him or her to perform the behavior?
- Has this behavior been taught in a concrete, sequential manner?
- Has the student practiced the appropriate behavior with success in this environment?
- Has the behavior been practiced in a variety of settings?
- What are other students doing when this behavior occurs?

Sometimes the answer lies between the student's challenges and the environmental challenges. One strategy to use when a new inappropriate behavior emerges is the ABCs of behavior management. The ABC method requires that the student is observed in the environment where the behavior has been occurring. Three elements of the behavior are analyzed:

A = Antecedent—what happens just before the behavior occurs?

B = Behavior—what is the exact behavior of the student?

C = Consequence—what happens just after the behavior?

For example, Bobby is making noise that bothers the student with ASD. Jamal (the student with ASD) wants to ask him to stop but doesn't know how other than to hit Bobby. Bobby complains to the teacher, and then Jamal gets punished by being made to sit alone.

The antecedent: Bobby makes noise.

The behavior: Jamal hits Bobby.

The consequence: Jamal gets punished

Potential long-term consequence: Student learns that hitting the peer gets him a reward: he is removed from the annoying noise!

It is important to understand that many behaviors are forms of communication. If educators, family, and peers can determine the antecedent, the behavior (intended message), and the common consequence, specific plans can be developed to teach the student the appropriate behavior when the antecedent happens again. Sometimes the antecedent is not easy to identify (e.g., student reacts to a certain smell or sound that is undetected by the observer). In the case of the example with Bobby and Jamal, the teachers identified the antecedent. Knowing the antecedent, the teachers could design a plan to teach Jamal the specific behavior of asking Bobby to stop making the noise (replacing the hitting behavior) and later teach the behavior in relationship to other students who make noise.

Most behaviors can be analyzed using the ABC technique. However, given the characteristics of ASD, there may be some inappropriate behaviors that do not readily fit into the ABC method of analysis. Such behaviors should be analyzed from the student's perspective. Knowing the student's perspective or the message of the behavior will help define what the student needs to know and be able to do to engage in positive behavior.

For example, say a student refuses to enter the auditorium.

- *Possible reasons:* The student may be sensitive to noise, crowds, being closed in, or new situations. The student may not understand the change. The student may associate the auditorium with a frightening experience.

To consider another example, say a student with ASD stays on the edge of groups, not joining in.

- *Possible reasons:* The student may have trouble initiating, especially with groups of people. The student may not be comfortable with the changing interaction patterns within a group.

Teach the Appropriate Replacement Behavior

It is important when attempting to stop an inappropriate behavior that students are also taught the replacement behavior. Most students will continue to demonstrate inappropriate behaviors unless taught an appropriate behavior to replace the inappropriate one. It is important to teach the student self-monitoring strategies and to help diffuse situations so that learning can take place. Students with ASD need to learn relaxation routines and to ask to be alone, to have their mentors and advocates identified, and to get help to access the supports that work.

Specific Behaviors of Concern

Three specific behaviors sometimes demonstrated by students with ASD are of concern in any learning environment: aggression, non-compliance, and tantrums. However, it is important to understand that the reason or purpose for the behavior will be different for each student due to the uniqueness of risk factors and protective factors.

Aggression (Hitting, Kicking, Biting, and Shoving)

Aggression is of major concern to everyone. In society, a person who is aggressive is at risk of being labeled as noncompliant, may be misunderstood, and may even be incarcerated. Aggression toward others is not permissible. However, the aggressive behavior of a student with ASD must be analyzed and the meaning of the behavior hypothesized from the student's perspective. Ask: "Why did the student use this behavior?" "What message is the student trying to convey?" and "Why did the student use this behavior to convey the message?"

Sometimes students used various methods in an attempt to make people understand that they did not like something, that they wanted someone to move, or that someone took something from them. In this case, they used aggression as their *last* resort. At other times, aggression is the first and only means the student uses to convey a message. Here are critical questions to ask initially:

- What primary challenges for this student hinder development of more appropriate means to have his or her messages understood?
- Does the student have sensory problems that are beyond tolerance level?
- Does the student need to finish something and become upset if interrupted?
- Does the student have the means to communicate wants and needs so everyone understands?
- Do the people in the environment respond to the appropriate means of communication when used?
- Are positive interaction patterns established between the student and peers?
- Are there activities the student can do with others?
- Are lots of negative messages delivered to this student?
- Can this student entertain herself?
- Can the student defend himself?

- Does the student see others engage in this type of behavior?
- Are there clear expectations, and are they applied consistently?
- Are there health problems?

Also, ask this question: What behavior does this student need to learn to replace the inappropriate behavior?

- To ask someone to stop or move?
- To ask someone for help?
- To tell someone no?
- To learn what activities and rules are negotiable and which are not?
- To learn to wait?
- To learn to take turns?
- To learn when some things aren't possible?
- To accept changes with accurate prior information?
- To accept the answers of others?
- To tell someone he does not feel well?

And ask: How can the student be taught new behaviors?

- Decide on the exact words and cues that will be used to teach the student.
- Provide multiple opportunities to model the new behavior.
- Reinforce the student for using the more appropriate behavior.
- Respond and react positively to the new behavior.

Finally, develop a plan for what to do when the behavior occurs:

- Set a plan that everyone uses when the behavior occurs.
- Avoid giving the behavior too much attention.
- Show what behavior is appropriate.

Noncompliance

Noncompliance is defined as when students do something they know they should not do or refuse to do something that someone wants them to do. Noncompliance is very difficult and annoying. However, it is often part of the student's attempt to exert independence and gain control. Adults need to avoid battles by making the rules absolutely clear. It should be clear to the student which rules are negotiable and which rules are not negotiable. To do this, educators, family, and peers must be sure of these rules themselves. Consistency in applying the rules is vital. When new rules and expectations are imposed, the student must be taught, desensitized, and rehearsed when necessary. Accurate, prior information that is understandable must be provided.

To understand the noncompliance behavior and determine the appropriate replacement behavior, ask: What is the purpose of the behavior from the student's perspective?

- Does the student know the rules, or do rules change depending on the person and the situation? Is there really consistency?
- Can the student do what is being asked? What would help the student comply?
- Is the student using this behavior as a way to interact?
- Does the student have choice and control over parts of the day at school?
- Is the student reinforced for following rules and doing as someone wants him to do?
- Does behaving appropriately earn attention meaningful rewards, or is behaving just expected and, thus, overlooked?
- Are sensory issues involved?
- Does the student know what is going to happen next and feel comfortable about it?

In addition, ask this question: What puts the student at risk for not being able to learn appropriate behaviors?

- Not understanding interactions and being successful with them?
- Not being able to communicate wants and needs well?
- Not being listened to and understood?
- A small repertoire of activities and interests?
- Sensory issues?
- Learning and attention problems?
- Anxiety and fears?

And ask: What does the student need so as not to engage in this behavior?

- To learn to get attention in a more direct way?
- To learn and practice the rules in a consistent way?
- To learn to communicate wants and needs directly—to have choices?
- To have more interesting things to do?
- To learn to wait?

- To learn to follow a visual sequence and predict what is coming next?
- To have more activities and interests to be redirected or directed to do?

Finally, develop a plan for what to do when the student engages in the behaviors:

- Follow a set plan with well-established procedures. When a student refuses to comply, a set format can be followed. For example, one might move closer, say the student's name, keep one's voice calm and direct, repeat the direction, then pause. Do this one more time but add, "I'll count to three, then I'll help you." Count at a set pace, using numbers that are visual; then help the student. Make sure the student knows the rule by practicing the rule several times.

Tantrums

Tantrums can disrupt the flow of learning and simple procedures such as moving through a lunch line. Typically, tantrums are used by students to refuse a request, a person, or an item. For example, a student may throw a tantrum when asked to work with a student he or she does not like. Tantrums, like other behaviors, are messages from the student. As with aggression and noncompliance, tantrums can be analyzed by asking certain questions.

What does the behavior mean from the student's point of view?

- Why is the student refusing?
- Is the student afraid, overwhelmed, or overstimulated?
- Is the pace too fast for the student or too slow?
- Are there too many demands?
- Are there sensory issues? Is the student tired or sick?
- Is the student lacking the necessary skills to cope with the situation?
- Does the student have more appropriate means to refuse, and are these behaviors "allowed" and responded to? Is the student responding to refusal?
- What does the student need to learn? A more appropriate way to refuse?
- Will saying no be acknowledged, or does the student need to use stronger behavior to get a point across?
- Will an appropriate way to refuse be acknowledged and honored?

Consider how to make refused activities more acceptable and motivating:

- Which activities are choices and which are not? Is this clear?
- Can the student make choices? Are there opportunities for choice?
- What is the value or motivation to comply?
- Are there too many rules?
- Are the rules clear and appropriate?

Other Possible Reasons for Problem Behaviors

Health Issues

Since many students with ASD are not able to convey accurately that they are not feeling well, this factor must always be considered. Constipation, toothaches, headaches, colds and flu, earaches, seizures, ulcers, allergies, appendicitis, and other conditions must be investigated and ruled out. This is especially true if there is a sudden change in the student's behavior or there doesn't appear to be any logical message behind the behavior. Sometimes, students use having a stomach ache or not feeling well as an escape. They have learned that this is an acceptable way to get help in anxious situations. If this appears to be the case, analyze the source of the anxiety carefully to provide the support needed.

General Everyday Issues

Being tired, hungry, and needing to be hugged or to be alone can also cause problems for a student who cannot initiate or negotiate well and does not do well with social interaction patterns.

Sensory Issues

Most students with ASD have reactions to sensory stimuli that are different from other people. Their reactions may vary from time to time. They may tune in to some things that the rest of us do not. They may need to explore their environments in various ways. They may have some problems knowing how their bodies relate to the environment or may need to move more. Whatever it is, they often are not able to advocate for this need directly, so it is important to pay attention to their reactions.

Are the same standards of discipline that are applied to students who are not disabled applied to a student with ASD?

The IEP committee determines, on an individual basis, if a student with a disability will follow the school's standard discipline codes. If the IEP committee determines that the student will not follow the standard discipline codes, a unique set of discipline codes is developed and noted on the IEP and within the conference summary report. The IEP committee describes precisely what discipline codes the student will be held accountable for while in school.

Given the nature of ASD, it is likely that some students will have discipline codes that vary from the school's code to some degree. However, it is important to understand that the decision of discipline is made by the IEP committee on an *individual basis* for each student. No one alternate discipline code works for every student with ASD. Just like every other aspect of the student's learning environment, discipline will be unique and based upon the strengths and needs of the student.

Conclusion

Each student with ASD is unique, and as the student grows up, there will be unique challenges. Teaching appropriate behavior is vital to the person's quality of life. However, the uniqueness of each student requires people to accept some behaviors that may seem a bit odd at times. The student may have unique ways to calm down and keep anxiety levels in check. The student may engage in these behaviors without regard to who is around or location. This requires teaching the student where to engage in the behaviors, how not to be quite so conspicuous while engaging in the behaviors, or a more acceptable behavior to accomplish the same purpose. The need for and the purpose of the behavior should be accepted and acknowledged.

Tolerance of differences and acceptance of behaviors that are unique should be fostered. A student with ASD is often corrected so much that the world seems rigid and intolerable. Channeling behaviors, accounting for special needs, and fostering strengths and interests while building skills and successful experiences are the cornerstone of helping the student grow and learn successfully. Emphasizing cooperative, rather than competitive, activities and cherishing the strengths of each student will build a community of learners who help one another.

As a team, parents, educators, and peers hope to broaden the student's world and people's understanding of ASD. The more people who understand ASD, the better the supports for students with ASD, which will help these students behave appropriately and flourish.

16

Facilitating Inclusion

Inclusion refers not merely to setting but to specially designed instruction and support for students with special needs in regular classrooms and neighborhood schools. Instruction, rather than setting, is the key to success, and decisions related to the placement of students are best made on an individual basis in a manner that maximizes their opportunity to participate fully in the experience of schooling. Inclusion is also called "integration" or "mainstreaming." There is much evidence to suggest that students with ASD can benefit from integration with typical peers.

Teacher Preparation

One of the most effective ways teachers can prepare for the inclusion of a student with ASD is to develop an understanding about the disorder by obtaining accurate information. Having access to accurate information fosters understanding and facilitates a positive attitude toward the challenge of including a student with ASD.

It is also important to gain knowledge about effective inclusion strategies. This can be achieved through reading, seeking out professional development experiences, and talking to or observing teachers with experience teaching students with ASD in integrated settings. Students with ASD constitute a diverse group, so it is important to acquire as much information about the individual student as possible.

Being proactive and anticipating potential problems increases the likelihood of successful inclusion. This involves identifying potential difficulties the student may encounter in the classroom and developing strategies to deal with or avoid such issues. Teachers also need to develop ways to facilitate peer interactions, consider behavioral issues, and develop support plans.

Students with ASD have unique patterns of learning. It is not unusual for them to forget previously learned concepts and skills. Similarly, students with ASD may be able to demonstrate a skill in one setting or on one task but not others. What may seem like noncompliance or stubbornness may be a manifestation of neurological and/or learning differences. While an uneven pattern of learning is a common feature of ASD, each student is unique. It is important to base expectations both on knowledge of the disorder and on knowledge of an individual student's strengths and needs.

The inclusion of students with ASD is the collective responsibility of teachers, teacher assistants, school administrators, school district consultants, and parents. All partners must work together for the experience to be successful.

The following suggestions may help teachers prepare to receive a student with ASD:

- Identify potential resources and sources of support.
- Seek the advice of experienced teachers.
- Set reasonable and achievable goals.
- Use existing or published resources (e.g., social scripts, visual supports). Individualizing programs does not necessarily mean developing all materials from scratch.
- Remember that even well-documented, evidence-based, and widely used strategies do not work with all students.
- Clearly define the roles of all staff working with the student.

Preparing Students With ASD

Competent social skills are essential to successful inclusion. However, it is unrealistic to postpone integration until the student has developed all of the prerequisite social skills. It is important to acknowledge that some students who would benefit from inclusion may take several years to develop even basic peer interaction skills.

In the home and preschool environments, teachers and parents can prepare students for inclusion by increasing their awareness of and interest in peers. It is often helpful to point out peers who are engaging in activities that may be of interest to children with ASD. Integration offers a wide variety of behaviors, skills, and attitudes to imitate and incorporate into existing skill sets. Consequently, enhancement of the student's imitation skills is an important component of programs for students with ASD.

Promoting Understanding

The most effective way to promote understanding and acceptance in the classroom is to model these positive attitudes. Students tend to perceive students with special needs as valued and equal members of the class when teachers do the following:

- Recognize students' achievements in meaningful ways.
- Call on students to participate in ways that are meaningful to them.
- Communicate that teasing and bullying are not acceptable and will not be tolerated.
- Adapt the program to allow all students to participate and learn.

It is human nature to be curious about and cautious of those who are different. Providing students with information can satisfy this curiosity. There are many ways to teach students about ASD. These include reading books, facilitating class discussions, showing videos, and/or inviting guest speakers to talk to the class. Parents can be effective and powerful guest speakers to invite into the classroom. Have students with ASD create an "All About Me" book or give short presentations about their strengths to share with classmates. Decisions about the amount and type of information to present should be made in consultation with students and their parents. The information should be comprehensive enough to address pertinent questions and dispel misconceptions but limited enough to respect students' privacy.

Respond to questions raised in class in an honest, open manner and address any incorrect assumptions and fears.

The following are common questions classmates ask:

- How did the student get ASD?
- Can I catch ASD?

- What can I do to help?
- Will the student get better?
- Why does the student do that (questions about specific behaviors)?

In some cases, parents express concern about having a student with ASD placed in their child's classroom. It can be helpful to explain how inclusion can be beneficial for typical students. Opportunities to interact with students with exceptional needs can promote understanding and acceptance. Inclusion should not adversely affect the quality of other students' education, nor should it significantly reduce the amount of teacher attention each student receives.

Several books and programs foster disability awareness and understanding. The activities generally highlight what it is like to live with a disability and conclude that all people have strengths and limitations. Ask students to communicate messages to each other without using words to help them experience what life is like for students with ASD. Or ask students to complete simple tasks wearing mittens or oven mitts. Or ask them to follow verbal instructions in another language or while wearing earplugs to sensitize them to obstacles faced by their classmate with ASD. To promote empathy, ask students to describe the feelings they experienced when visiting foreign lands or in unfamiliar situations.

Adapting Instruction

One way to facilitate acceptance and understanding is to adapt instruction to ensure all students have access to programs of study. Decisions regarding adaptations should consider students' skills and abilities and the topics being taught. In some cases, it may not be necessary to adapt lessons at all. In other situations, it may be necessary to provide supports such as peer partners for students to be successful. Alternatively, it may be necessary to adapt the lesson or classroom activity. Adaptations can range from relatively minor (e.g., adjusting the size of the task) to major (e.g., altering the content or difficulty level). In some cases, programming may involve individualized functional goals that are addressed within the classroom.

Adapting Equipment

In some situations, it may be necessary to adapt classroom materials to increase the likelihood of success. The following is a list of possible equipment adaptations:

- Grip adapters may be required for pencils, spoons, and tooth-brushes for students who display fine motor difficulties.
- Raised-line paper creates a more obvious physical boundary and can help students print between lines.
- Some students display a high level of motor restlessness and have a difficult time inhibiting movement for extended periods of time. In such situations, inflated seat cushions may have a positive impact on their ability to attend. Similarly, some students are more attentive when seated on a therapy ball.
- Zipper extensions and/or shoes with Velcro closures may allow students to dress independently.
- Students who experience great difficulty with fine motor tasks may be more successful using computers to complete written assignments. Some students respond positively to early literacy software.
- Adapted scissors may help students cut paper more effectively and independently.
- Spatial concepts, such as left and right, are often difficult for students with ASD to understand. It may be helpful to mark shoes in an unobtrusive manner to ensure they are placed on the correct foot.
- Some students become distracted by irrelevant information (e.g., page numbers, lines, pictures). It may be necessary to eliminate extraneous details from books and worksheets.
- Some students find glossy surfaces distracting. It may be necessary to adapt books and desktops to give surfaces a matte finish.

Occupational therapists are an excellent resource for ideas on how to adapt equipment to ensure students with ASD experience success.

Adapting the Physical Environment

Given that many students with ASD display difficulty self-modulating sensory information, it is important to consider which areas within the classroom are most conducive to learning. If students tend to overreact to auditory stimulation, it may be unwise to have them sit near the door. Similarly, students who have a difficult time coping with fluorescent lighting may experience more success when seated by a window. If students are preoccupied with computers or the alphabet, it may be beneficial to position their desks so these items are not visible. Many students with ASD have relatively subtle sensory issues. For instance, if a student is sensitive to certain smells, he or she may have a difficult time attending to structured tasks when sitting near peers wearing perfume or cologne.

In some situations, it can be helpful to define the physical space associated with a particular activity in a concrete manner. For example, students with ASD may be more successful during group activities that are completed on the floor if a specific space is defined for them. Mats or squares can be provided for all students to avoid drawing attention to an individual student. Alternatively, if a student has a difficult time concentrating when peers are present in the immediate environment, it may be helpful to assign the locker or coat hook at the end of a row.

Adapting Evaluation Methods

Existing evaluation and report card formats may not have the flexibility or capacity to provide relevant information on the progress and learning of a student with ASD. It may be necessary to develop a separate system to measure progress and communicate this information. Prior to introducing a new unit or concept, it is important for teachers to determine how students with ASD will be expected to demonstrate learning. For instance, it may be necessary to make the following adaptations:

- Test recognition skills (multiple-choice tests) versus recall skills (tests that require students to generate correct answers).
- Specify the amount of supervision or prompting required for specific tasks.
- Reduce the length of tests.
- Give oral tests.
- Allow students to use tools, such as dictionaries, counting blocks, or calculators.
- Evaluate skills based on observation of performance.
- Complete baselines and postteaching skill checklists to assess skill development.

Adapting Assignments

Students with ASD often require more time than their classmates to process verbal information and initiate responses. This difficulty is often compounded when fine motor skills are delayed. When new concepts are introduced or relatively difficult tasks are presented, it may be helpful to present students with shorter or condensed versions of the task. For example, if the class assignment involves a worksheet with ten math questions, present students with ASD with five questions. This type of adaptation stresses the importance of quality, not quantity. As students experience success, the length of tasks should be gradually increased so they complete the same amount of work as their peers.

Adapting Input Methods

Given that impaired communication skills are a hallmark of the disorder, it is not surprising that an effective way to adapt tasks for students with ASD is to alter the way instructions and lessons are delivered. Reduce the length or complexity of instructions. The simple statement "Get your math book," may be easier to comprehend than "Now it is time to turn our attention to the world of math; get out your materials." Because some students display attention difficulties, they often have a difficult time attending to and remembering verbal instructions. It is often helpful to provide students with written instructions to refer to throughout activities. Some students respond better when words are printed in a relatively large font.

Students with ASD tend to be visual learners, and in many situations, "a picture is worth a thousand words." Providing visual supports to augment learning activities or instructions is often effective. This may involve bridging written words or instructions with pictures, providing pictures alone, or actually modeling specific tasks or steps. Rather than showing the class a finished class project and verbally explaining the steps involved, it may be more effective to model each step of the process. Or it may be possible to call upon a peer to model the steps.

Adapting Output Methods

The verbal skills of students with ASD are often significantly delayed, so it is often necessary to adapt how students are expected to respond to questions and assignments. Consider these adaptations:

- Print, rather than write, responses.
- Give single-word responses rather than phrases or sentences.
- Type responses rather than printing them.
- Circle correct responses rather than printing them.

- Copy responses rather than working from memory.
- Point to responses rather than answering questions verbally.
- Provide picture symbol responses rather than verbal answers.
- Draw pictures rather than print responses.
- Develop collages rather than stories or paragraphs.

Modifying Content and Difficulty Levels

It is sometimes necessary to modify the content or difficulty level of learning activities to suit better the interests and learning needs of students with ASD. This type of modification can take many forms. Because these students often have difficulty comprehending abstract concepts, it may be necessary to present concepts in a concrete manner. For instance, the concepts of *public* and *private* are relatively abstract. For students to grasp these concepts, it may be necessary to present concrete examples and explanations of each. This could be achieved using words, pictures, or real-life experiences.

Concept maps can also be used to make abstract concepts understandable. They allow a group of students to work on the same project at a variety of different levels. Generally, the main concept is outlined in the middle of the map using words or pictures. Lines are then drawn to connect related facts or concepts. Each concept is defined using words, hand-drawn pictures, or photographs cut from magazines. Concept maps are often helpful as they result in a concrete visual representation of a pertinent topic or issue. They also allow students with ASD to participate actively in group projects.

Some students with ASD resist tasks that are not meaningful to them. It is often helpful to incorporate students' interests into lessons. For instance, if a student displays a strong interest in dinosaurs, ask the student to print out dinosaur names instead of completing the printing exercise the rest of the class is working on. Similarly, providing the student with a dinosaur book during free reading periods may increase the student's level of participation. Although the ultimate goal of programming is to broaden the student's interests, incorporating preferred topics into learning activities can promote skill development and increase motivation. Adding a sensory element to activities can also motivate some students. For instance, printing letters in sand or forming them out of play dough can make printing more appealing.

Students with ASD tend to be more motivated when activities have a distinct purpose they understand. Counting blocks for the sake of counting blocks may not seem meaningful, but counting how many students are present in the classroom and taking attendance information to the office may seem more purposeful. Similarly, printing out random words may not be motivating, but printing out their daily schedules or the lunch menu may be more meaningful. Presenting learning activities in a game format can also increase interest in participation. For example, if the topic is "community helpers," it might be possible to develop a bingo game for students (e.g., "This person keeps the community safe by putting out fires.")

Promoting Organization

Some students with ASD have a difficult time keeping their materials organized and retrieving them when required. They may also miss out on important verbal instructions. As a result, they experience anxiety because other students are ahead of them. One way to avoid these problems is to help students develop effective organizational strategies. Following are some possibilities:

- Color code materials and associate each color with a particular subject on the student's daily schedule (e.g., math is red, spelling is blue).
- Place labels or pictures in students' lockers or desks to indicate where materials should be placed.
- Provide students with tubs or bags to store materials associated with a particular subject.
- Provide agendas or checklists to ensure students are aware of all assignments and deadlines.
- Help students ensure that their binders are organized in an effective manner.
- Provide students with visual checklists to ensure that specific routines are completed (e.g., putting required materials into backpacks at the end of the day).

Some students require assistance to organize their thoughts effectively. They tend to benefit from strategies such as making outlines and concept maps.

One-to-One Instruction

Leaving the classroom for one-to-one tutoring or therapy is one instructional option that teachers and parents may consider. In some cases, such tutoring can occur within the classroom environment (e.g., in a quiet corner). The main consideration in determining whether pull-out time is necessary is "Can this concept or topic be taught effectively in a group environment?" If the answer is yes, then providing isolated instruction may not be warranted. Classroom teachers should make decisions regarding pull-out time after carefully considering individual students' needs and consulting with parents and other team members.

Some students with ASD learn more efficiently when environmental distractions are minimized and/or when they receive direct one-to-one teaching. Therefore, pull-out time may be necessary when new concepts or relatively difficult concepts are introduced. Also, some students experience significant levels of anxiety when they make errors in front of their peers. In such cases, pull-out time allows students to practice skills without an audience. In some situations, it is difficult to adapt a particular lesson, so it can be more efficient to work outside the classroom.

When pull-out instruction is necessary, it is critical that learning activities within and outside the classroom be coordinated to promote skill development and generalization. Students need to learn to benefit from group learning experiences and attend to classroom teachers. One alternative to pull-out time is to create groupings of students with similar skill sets and provide small-group instruction.

Promoting Positive Peer Interactions

A concerted effort must be made to help students with ASD refine their social skills and to provide peers with the skills and knowledge they need to interact successfully with classmates who have ASD. Students need opportunities that promote positive interactions. Adult assistance should be deliberately faded to allow students to interact as naturally as possible. Peers are often discouraged from talking to a student who is working with the teacher assistant, so students with ASD are sometimes isolated if they may spend considerable time working with teacher assistants.

Refining the social skills of students with ASD should be a primary and ongoing educational goal. Different interventions and teaching approaches are required by different students in different situations. In some cases, it may be necessary to teach critical social skills during pull-out time or by creating a small grouping of students. Social scripts and stories can also be developed to help students negotiate their way through specific social situations. Teaching staff can also provide students with social coaching. This can involve "coaching from the sidelines" while interactions are occurring or by debriefing with students after interactions.

Classmates frequently misinterpret the behavior or mannerisms of students with ASD. For example, it is common for peers to assume that students with ASD are unfriendly when they do not respond to questions or greetings. Some students assume that echolalia is intended to mock others or that it is a result of "being allowed to do whatever they want to." It is important to help peers develop insight into the possible causes or functions of the behaviors students with ASD often display. Dispelling myths can help peers become more accepting.

It is also helpful to give peers specific instructions about how to interact with students with ASD. Peers are often reticent to interact with students with special needs for fear that they will say or do something wrong. The best way to overcome this fear is to provide students with accurate information and practical suggestions:

- Encourage peers to be gently persistent during interactions. They should repeat questions and comments and not give up prematurely.
- Encourage classmates to offer cues and assistance rather than giving answers to students with ASD.
- Coach peers to provide adequate time for students with ASD to process information before making additional comments.
- Provide concrete suggestions about ways to respond to specific behaviors and/or situations. For example, peers should be told what to do if a student engages in potentially dangerous behavior, displays aggression, fails to follow the rules of a game, has a seizure, etc. Dealing with negative behaviors should never be the responsibility of peers.
- Explain how students with ASD communicate (e.g., word approximations, sign language, picture symbols, and gestures) to facilitate understanding.
- Encourage peers to incorporate visuals when communicating with students with ASD.
- Encourage peers to make sure students with ASD are attending before asking questions or making comments.
- Tell peers that it is acceptable to say "no" or "stop" when students display inappropriate behaviors.

In some situations, it may be useful to enlist a specific peer or a small group of peers to help students with ASD develop peer-interaction skills. Select mature peers who display high levels of self-confidence and strong social skills. Once peers have been enlisted, they should be provided with specific roles and responsibilities. It is often helpful to assign play buddies so students with ASD can participate in recess activities. It may be possible to assign study buddies for certain classroom activities. Regardless of the roles they are asked to assume, it is important to remember that peer coaches require ongoing support and encouragement.

Consider creating opportunities to facilitate peer interactions in the classroom. When activities are completed in defined physical spaces, peers are in close proximity to one another and less likely to spread out and form subgroups. It can also be beneficial to create situations that allow students with ASD to demonstrate their strengths to classmates. Students often respond positively when they are placed in situations where they are more able or skilled than their partners. Ask students to read to younger students or tutor students in subject areas they have mastered. Facilitate peer interactions by planning cooperative learning activities that require group members to work together. To maximize effectiveness, each member of the group should be assigned a role consistent with her skills.

Forming teams and partners can be anxiety provoking for students with ASD, particularly for those students who are aware that they are less able or different from their peers. Use creative ways to pair up students and form teams. For example, it may be possible to form teams or partners on the basis of height, month of birth, color of eyes, or favorite sports team or by lottery. Such methods ensure students have opportunities to partner with a number of different peers.

17

Transition Planning for Students With ASD

Individuals with ASD frequently have difficulty with the unknown and may fear the unpredictable. It is difficult for them to take in all of the information within a new situation, determine what the expectations are, and then generate appropriate responses. As a result, transitions are often difficult for individuals with ASD and Asperger syndrome and may result in increased anxiety and inappropriate or resistant behaviors.

It is not possible to provide a program and environment that are free from transitions and free from change; they are a part of life. The goal is to help the student cope with the changes and to adapt to a variety of settings. In many situations, anxiety can be decreased and inappropriate behaviors prevented or reduced if the individual is prepared for change and transition. This includes transitions between activities and settings throughout the day, transitions from one grade to the next, transition from one school to another, and transition to adult life.

Transitions Between Activities and Settings

- Give the student ample warning prior to any transition.
- Schedules can be used to prepare the student for changes in activities. It is important to involve the student in referring to

the schedule. This can be done at the beginning of the day, as well as at transition times.

- Outline the schedule using a description of what to expect (e.g., first _____, then _____).
- Schedules vary in terms of complexity and length and are tailored to the ability of the individual student. They can be presented in written words, pictures/pictographs, or objects that depict certain activities. It is important to implement a method that indicates the completion of an activity, such as turning over a picture card or crossing out an activity.
- A schedule may not be sufficient to prepare the student for change. In some situations, teachers have provided the student with an object that will be used in the next activity or setting to help him understand what is coming next.
- The use of a watch, clock, or timer may help the student to understand time periods.
- Social stories are effective in preparing some students for change and particularly for preparing students for new situations and unfamiliar activities.
- The use of visual cues in combination with verbal instructions may help the student to understand what is expected.
- Allow choice whenever possible.

Transitions Between Grade Levels

- When preparing for the transition between classrooms, it is necessary to prepare the student and the receiving teacher. Preparation for transition should begin in early spring.
- The receiving teacher must be provided with information about the student's strengths and needs. This can be facilitated through team meeting(s) involving teachers, parents, support personnel, and the teacher assistant(s). The receiving teacher may also need to be provided with information about ASD and the educational implications.
- It is beneficial for the receiving teacher to visit the student in the current classroom environment to observe the child's participation as well as the current instructional strategies that are effective for the student.
- The student can be prepared for the new classroom setting through the use of social stories and photographs of the new teacher and classroom. It may be helpful to prepare a small scrapbook that the student can refer to over the summer.

- The student may also make visits to the future classroom. It may be helpful for the student to be accompanied by the teacher assistant or current teacher to maintain some familiarity.
- It is also possible to prepare the student with the use of videotapes of the new setting.

A planning meeting is conducted to exchange information about the student as well as to discuss instructional strategies and approaches that have been most effective. Ideally, the meeting involves parents, teachers, teacher assistant, speech language pathologist, and others who are involved in the child's program on an ongoing basis. This provides the parents and teachers with the opportunity to discuss goals, instructional strategies, curricular modifications, methods for maintaining appropriate behavior, and communication. It is preferable to conduct the meeting before the end of the current school year. However, some teachers prefer to have additional time to get to know the student. If the receiving teacher has had opportunity to meet and observe the student in the current classroom, and if information regarding strengths, needs, and recommended strategies has been exchanged, it is feasible to conduct the planning meeting in the fall.

Transitions Between Schools

The suggestions for transitions between classrooms are also applicable to planning for transitions between schools. However, additional time and preparation may be required, as the student will need to adjust to a whole new building rather than just a classroom. If the transition is from elementary to high school, the student will also need to learn about changes in the way school operates. For example, the student will need to be prepared for the number of teachers that he or she will have and the various locations for instruction.

- Arrange for the student to visit the school on a number of occasions. If the student is particularly resistant to change, it may be necessary to introduce new aspects slowly and to go through a process of desensitization and rehearsal. For example, the initial visit may need to be devoted to simply going to the school and going in the front door. On another visit, the student might visit a classroom, then the gymnasium, and later individual classrooms.
- Providing the student with a videotape of the new school and written information (appropriate to the student's academic level) may help the student to rehearse for the change.

- Identify key people whom the student can talk to or go to for help.
- Identify peers who may help the student adjust to the new school and who may be able to accompany the student to various locations in the school.

Transition From High School to Adult Life

It is recommended that transition planning from high school to adult life begin as early as possible. The student and parents need time to make the adjustment from elementary school to secondary school. Then formal planning for transition to adult life often begins after the first year of secondary school. Although it may seem that there is ample time to postpone transition planning until the last year or two of secondary school, it is important that parents, advocates, school personnel, and adult service providers begin to consider long-term planning for the individual in the following areas:

- Graduation or school exit date
- Employment options
- Postsecondary training/education
- Income support/insurance
- Residential options
- Transportation needs
- Medical needs
- Community recreation and leisure options
- Maintenance of family/friend relationships
- Advocacy/guardianship

Transition planning is a shared responsibility among the parent/guardian(s), the school, and adult service providers. Likewise, to be effective, the planning process for transition should be a collaborative effort among the student, family, school, and adult service providers. The identification of desired postschool outcomes is the driving force behind transition planning, so the student and family are central to the planning process.

Regardless of the process or format used to conduct the transition planning meeting, the end result should be a section of the student's personal program plan that targets desired outcomes for adult life, specific current needs, a plan for addressing those needs, identification of the agencies/persons responsible, and time lines. Subsequent planning meetings will need to be arranged to review the plan and to check that specific objectives have been achieved, that the long-term goals are still appropriate, and that necessary revisions are made (Freeze, 1995).

The role of school personnel is to continue to provide opportunities for the student to develop skills for work and independent living. The day-to-day program and instruction for the student increasingly focus on developing functional skills and community-based training.

The range of expectations will depend on the student's ability and needs. For example, some students with Asperger syndrome may plan to go on to further education following secondary school. Consequently, there will be a greater emphasis on academic preparation in addition to work experience, as well as development of job-related skills and skills for leisure and recreation. For others, the program may focus on work experience, community-based training, and self-care.

In general, the school program prepares the student for transition in the following ways:

- Providing a variety of work experiences to help the individual determine preferences
- Encouraging participation in extracurricular activities and social events
- Encouraging volunteer work
- Helping with developing a resume
- Training in social skills for the job place
- Teaching appropriate dress and hygiene
- Providing on-the-job preparation, once preferences have been established
- Training in the use of public transportation
- Training in self-care
- Training in self-management
- Teaching functional academics appropriate to the ability level of the student

References and Suggested Readings

American Academy of Pediatrics, Committee of Children with Disabilities. (1998). Auditory integration training and facilitated communication for ASD. *Pediatrics, 120*(2), 431–433.

American Psychiatric Association (APA). (1994). *Diagnostic and statistical manual of mental disorders* (4th ed.) (DSM-IV). Washington, DC: Author.

American Psychiatric Association (APA). (2000). *Diagnostic and statistical manual of mental disorders: Text revision* (4th ed.) (DSM-IV-TR). Washington, DC: Author.

Ayers, K., & Langone, J. (2005). Intervention and instruction with video for students with autism: A review of the literature. *Education and Training in Developmental Disabilities, 40*(2), 183–196.

Baranek, G. (2002). Efficacy of sensory and motor intervention for children with autism. *Journal of Autism and Developmental Disorders, 32*(5), 397–422.

Bock, S. J., & Myles, B. S. (1999). An overview of characteristics of Asperger syndrome. *Education and Training in Mental Retardation and Developmental Disabilities, 34*(4), 511–520.

Bowe, F. (2005). *Making inclusion work.* Upper Saddle River: Merrill Pearson.

Centers for Disease Control and Prevention (CDC). (2007a). *About autism.* Retrieved November 1, 2007, from www.cdc.gov/ncbddd/autism/

Centers for Disease Control and Prevention (CDC). (2007b). *Prevalence of autism.* Retrieved November 20, 2007, from www.cdc.gov/ncbddd/autism/faq_prevalence.htm

Charlop-Christy, M., & Daneshvar, S. (2003). Using video modeling to teach perspective taking to children with autism. *Journal of Positive Behavior Interventions, 5*(1), 12–21.

Charlop-Christy, M., Le, L., & Freeman, K. (2000). A comparison of video modeling with in vivo modeling for teaching children with autism. *Journal of Autism and Developmental Disorders, 30*(6), 537–552.

Charlop, M., & Milstein, J. (1989). Teaching autistic children conversational speech using video modeling. *Journal of Applied Behavior Analysis, 22,* 275–285.

Colarusso, R., & O'Rourke, C. (2004). *Special education for all teachers.* Dubuque: Kendall Hunt.

Cowley, G. (2000, July 31). The challenge of "mindblindness." *Newsweek,* 46–54.

Cullain, R. (2000). The effect of social stories on anxiety levels and excessive behavioral expressions of elementary school-aged children with autism (Doctoral dissertation, Union Institute and University, 2000). *Dissertation Abstracts International, 62,* 2383.

Dales, L., Hammer, S. J., & Smith, N. J. (2001). Time trends in autism and in MMR immunization coverage in California. *Journal of the American Medical Association, 285*(9), 1183–1185.

Davidovitch, M., Glick, L., Holtzman, G., Tirosh, E., & Safir, M. (2000). Developmental regression in autism: Maternal perception. *Journal of Autism and Developmental Disorders, 30*(2), 113–119.

Dawson, G., & Watling, R. (2000). Interventions to facilitate auditory, visual and motor integration in autism: A review of evidence. *Journal of Autism and Developmental Disorders, 30*(5), 415–421.

Deutsch-Smith, D. (2004). *Introduction to special education: Teaching in an age of opportunity* (5th ed.). Needham Heights, MA: Allyn & Bacon.

Freeze, D. (1995). *Promoting successful transition for students with special needs.* Arlington, VA: Canadian Council for Exceptional Children.

Friend, M. (2005). *Special education: Contemporary perspectives for school professionals.* Boston: Allyn & Bacon.

Gargiulio, R. M. (2004). *Special education in contemporary society: An introduction to exceptionality.* Belmont: Wadsworth-Thompson.

Gillberg, C., & Coleman, M. (2000). *The biology of the autistic syndromes* (3rd ed.). London: MacKeith.

Gray, C. A. (1995). Teaching children with ASD to "read" social situations. In K. A. Quill (Ed.), *Teaching children with ASD: Strategies to enhance communication and socialization* (pp. 219–242). Albany, NY: Delmar.

Greenspan, S., & Wieder, S. (1997). Developmental patterns and outcomes in infants and children with disorders in relating and communicating: A chart review of 200 cases of children with autistic spectrum diagnoses. *Journal of Developmental and Learning Disorders, 1,* 87–141.

Hallahan, D. P., & Kauffman, J. M. (2006). *Exceptional learners: An introduction to special education* (10th ed.). Boston: Allyn & Bacon.

Handleman, J., & Harris, S. (2000). *Preschool education program for children with autism* (2nd ed.). Austin, TX: ProEd.

Helfin, J., & Simpson, R. (1998). Interventions for children and youth with autism: Prudent choices in a world of exaggerated claims and empty promises. Part I: Intervention and treatment option review. *Focus on Autism and Other Developmental Disabilities, 13*(4), 194–211.

Herbert, J., Sharp, I., & Gaudiano, B. (2002). Separating fact from fiction in the etiology and treatment of autism. *The Scientific Review of Mental Health Practice, 1*(1), 23–43.

Heward, W. L. (2006). Exceptional children: An introduction to special education (8th ed.). Upper Saddle River, NJ: Pearson Education.

Howlin, P., Baron-Cohen, S. & Hadwin, J. (1998). *Teaching children with autism to mind-read: A practical guide.* Hoboken, NJ: Wiley.

Humphries, A. (2003). Effectiveness of PRT as a behavioral intervention for young children with ASD. *Bridges practice-based research syntheses, 2*(4), 1–10.

Individuals with Disabilities Education Act (IDEA), 34 C.F.R. § 300.8(c)(1) (2004).

Ingersoll, B., Dvortcsak, A., Whalen, C., & Sikora, D. (2005). The effects of a developmental, social-pragmatic language intervention on rate of expressive language production in young children with autism spectrum disorders. *Focus on Autism and Other Developmental Disabilities, 20*(4), 213–222.

International Molecular Genetics Study of Autism Consortium (IMGSAC). (1998). A full genome screen for autism with evidence for linkage to a region on chromosome 7q. *Human Molecular Genetics, 7*(3), 571–578.

International Rett Syndrome Foundation. (2005). *Introduction to Rett syndrome.* Retrieved June 10, 2005, from www.rsrf.org/about_rett_syndrome/

Kadesjo, B., Gillberg, C., & Hagberg, B. (1999). Brief report: ASD and Asperger syndrome in seven-year-old children; a total population study. *Journal of Autism and Developmental Disorders, 29,* 327–331.

Kliewer, C., & Biklen, D. (1996). Labeling: Who wants to be called retarded? In W. Stainback & S. Stainback (Eds.), *Controversial issues confronting special education: Divergent perspectives* (2nd ed., pp. 83–95). Boston: Allyn & Bacon.

Klingner, J. K., Vaughn, S., Schumm, J. S., Cohen, P., & Forgan, J. W. (1998). Inclusion or pullout: Which do students prefer? *Journal of Learning Disabilities, 31,* 148–158.

Koegel, R., & Koegel, L. (1995). *Teaching children with ASD: Strategies for initiating positive interactions and improving learning opportunities.* Baltimore: Brookes.

Konstantareas, M. M., & Homatidis, S. (1999). Chromosomal abnormalities in a series of children with autistic disorder. *Journal of Autism and Developmental Disorders, 29*(4), 275–285.

Kuoch, H., & Mirenda, P. (2003). Social story interventions for young children with autism spectrum disorders. *Focus on Autism and Other Developmental Disabilities, 18*(4), 219–227.

Kuttler, S., Myles, B., & Carlson, J. K. (1998). The use of social stories to reduce precursors to tantrum behavior in a student with autism. *Focus on Autism and Other Developmental Disabilities, 13*(3), 176–182.

LeBlanc, L., Coates, A., Daneshvar, S., Charlop-Christy, M., Morris, M., & Lancaster, B. (2003). Using video modeling and reinforcement to teach perspective-taking skills to children with autism. *Journal of Applied Behavior Analysis, 36*(2), 253–257.

Mayo Clinic. (2006). *Asperger's syndrome.* Retrieved January 20, 2008, from www.mayoclinic.com/health/aspergers-syndrome/DS00551

National Autistic Society. (2005). *Asperger syndrome: What is it?* Retrieved June 27, 2005, from www.nas.org.uk/nas/jsp/polopoly.jsp?d=212

National Dissemination Center for Children with Disabilities. (2007). *Autism and pervasive developmental disorder.* Retrieved November 4, 2007, from http://nichcy.org/pubs/factshe/fs1txt.htm

National Institute of Neurological Disorders and Stroke. (2005a). *Asperger syndrome fact sheet* (NIH Publication No. 05-5624). Bethesda, MD: Author.

National Institute of Neurological Disorders and Stroke. (2005c). *Rett syndrome information page.* Retrieved June 7, 2005, from www.ninds.nih.gov/disorders/rett/rett.htm

National Research Council. (2001). *Educating children with autism* (Committee on Educational Interventions for Children with Autism, Division of Behavioral and Social Sciences and Education). Washington, DC: National Academy Press.

Nemours Foundation. (2005). *Asperger syndrome.* Retrieved June 15, 2005, from http://kidshealth.org/parent/medical/brain/asperger.html

Norris, C., & Datillo, J. (1999). Evaluating effects of a social story on a young girl with autism. *Focus on Autism and Other Developmental Disabilities, 14*(3), 180–186.

Padeliadu, S., & Zigmond, N. (1996). Perspectives of students with learning disabilities about special education placement. *Learning Disabilities Research & Practice, 11*(1), 15–23.

Perry, A., & Condillac, R. (2003). Evidence-based practices for children and adolescents with autism spectrum disorders: Review of literature and practice guide. *Children's Mental Health Ontario.* Retrieved July 19, 2005, from www.kidsmentalhealth.ca/resources/evidence_based_practices.php

Pierangelo, R., & Giuliani, G. (2007). *EDM: The educator's diagnostic manual of disabilities and disorders.* San Francisco: Jossey Bass.

Prizant, B., & Wetherby, A. (1998). Understanding the continuum of discrete-trial traditional behavioral to social-pragmatic developmental approaches in communication enhancement for young children with ASD/PDD. *Seminars in Speech and Language, 19*(4), 329–348.

Rodier, P. (2000). The early origins of autism. *Scientific American, 282*(2), 56–63.

Schopler, E., & Reichler, R. J. (1971). Parents as co-therapists in the treatment of psychotic children. *Journal of Autism and Childhood Schizophrenia, 1,* 87–102.

Scott, F. J., Baron-Cohen, S., Bolton, P., & Brayne, C. (2002). Brief report: Prevalence of autism spectrum conditions in children aged 5–11 years in Cambridgeshire, UK. *Autism, 6*(3), 231–237.

Scott, J., Clark, C., & Brady, M. (2000). *Students with autism: Characteristics and instructional programming.* San Diego: Singular.

Shipley-Benamou, R., Lutzker, J., & Taubman, M. (2002). Teaching daily living skills to children with autism through instructional video modeling. *Journal of Positive Behavior Interventions, 4*(3), 166–177.

Simpson, R. (2005). Evidence-based practices and students with autism spectrum disorders. *Focus on Autism and Other Developmental Disabilities, 20*(3), 140–149.

Simpson, R., & Zionts, P. (2000). *Autism: Information and resources for professionals and parents* (2nd ed.). Austin, TX: Pro-Ed.

Stainback, W., & Stainback, S. (1990). Inclusive schooling. In W. Stainback & S. Stainback (Eds.), *Support networks for inclusive schooling* (pp. 51–63). Baltimore, MD: Brooks.

Stratton, K., Gable, A., Shetty, P., & McCormick, M. C. (Eds.). (2001). *Immunization safety review: Measles-mumps-rubella vaccine and autism.* Washington, DC: National Academy.

Swaggart, B. L., Gagnon, E., Bock, S. J., Earles, E. L., Quinn, C., Myles, B. S., et al. (1995). Using social stories to teach social & behavioral skills to children with autism. *Focus on Autistic Behavior, 10,* 1–15.

Szatmari, P., Jones, M. B., Zwaigenbaum, L., & MacLean, J. E. (1998). Genetics of autism: Overview and new directions. *Journal of Autism and Developmental Disorders, 28*(5), 351–368.

Technology-Related Assistance for Individuals with Disabilities Act of 1988, 29 U.S.C.A. § 2201 *et seq.*

Turnbull, A., Turnbull, R., & Wehmeyer, M. (2006). *Exceptional lives: Special education in today's schools* (5th ed.). Upper Saddle River: Pearson.

U.S. Department of Education. (2004). *The 26th annual report to Congress on the implementation of Individuals with Disabilities Education Act (IDEA).* Washington, DC: Author.

U.S. National Library of Medicine. (2004a). *Asperger syndrome.* Retrieved June 30, 2005, from www.nlm.nih.gov/medlineplus/ency/article/001549.htm

U.S. National Library of Medicine. (2004b). *Childhood disintegrative disorder.* Retrieved July 2, 2005, from www.nlm.nih.gov/medlineplus/ency/article/001535.htm

Vaughn, S., Bos, C., & Schumm, J. S. (2003). *Teaching exceptional and diverse at-risk students in the general education classroom* (3rd ed.). Boston: Allyn & Bacon.

Volkmar, F., Paul, R., Klin, A., & Cohen, D. (Eds.). (2005). *Handbook of autism and pervasive developmental disorders* (3rd ed., Vols. 1 & 2). Hoboken, NJ: Wiley & Sons.

Wagner, S. (1999). Inclusive programming for elementary students with autism. Arlington, TX: Future Horizons.

Wakefield, A. J., Murch, S. H., Anthony, A., Linnell, J., Casson, D. M., & Malik, M. (1998). Ileal-lymphoid-nodular hyperplasia, non-specific colitis and pervasive development disorder in children. *Lancet, 351,* 637–641.

Weiss, M., Wagner, S., & Bauman, M. (1996). A validated case study of facilitated communication. *Mental Retardation, 34*(4), 220–230.

Westling, D. L., & Fox, L. (2004). *Teaching students with severe disabilities* (3rd ed.). Upper Saddle River: Pearson.

World Health Organization (WHO). (1990). International Classification of Diseases (10th ed.) (ICD-10). Geneva, Switzerland: Author.

Yale Developmental Disabilities Clinic. (2005). *Childhood disintegrative disorder.* Retrieved April 3, 2006, from http://info.med.yale.edu/chldstdy/autism/cdd.html

Yirmiya, N., Shaked, M., & Erel, O. (2001). Comparison of siblings of individuals with autism and siblings of individuals with other diagnoses: An empirical summary. In E. Schopler, N. Yirmiya, C. Shulman, & L. Marcus (Eds.), *The research basis for autism intervention* (pp. 59–73). New York: Kluwer Academic/Plenum.

Index

The Corwin Press logo—a raven striding across an open book—represents the union of courage and learning. Corwin Press is committed to improving education for all learners by publishing books and other professional development resources for those serving the field of PreK–12 education. By providing practical, hands-on materials, Corwin Press continues to carry out the promise of its motto: **"Helping Educators Do Their Work Better."**